In Cons

Cats

KEITH BRAZIL

Keith Brazil

ISBN-13: 978-1-909598-10-2

DEDICATION

For Teresa

Some observations on cats and our fascination with
their fascination

To the cast of cats and characters of my observations:

Dinah (sister and mother)

Hector (brother and uncle)

Iolaus (son, step-brother, and nephew)

Willow (daughter, step-sister, and niece)

and their American assorted counter-parts

Fluffy, Kemp and Payton

Tigger, Angel and Trixie

"It is a fact, a simple fact, that you cannot distract a
cat from its singular attraction..." (KB)

"It is not for us to search but to remain still,

to achieve Immobility not Action..."

Wei Wu Wei

"Bagpuss, dear Bagpuss,

Old Fat Furry Catpus,

Wake up and look at this thing that I bring,

Wake up, be bright, be golden and light,

Bagpuss, oh hear what I sing…"

(Emily to Bagpuss)

CONTENTS

Acknowledgments   i

In Consideration of Cats   Page 1

ACKNOWLEDGMENTS

Illustrations & Cat Portraits: Colin Francolino-Scott

Additional sketches: Keith & Michael Brazil

Cover Design: Michael Brazil & Adam Wiltshire

Editor: Kitty Malone

With thanks to: Tony, Adam and Sean, Adrian, Paul E, Paul and Hendrik, Patricia and Michael Wood, Chris, Pauline and 'George the Cat'

Special thanks to: my family, Suki, Toby, Dinah, Hector, Iolaus, Willow, Teresa, Trish, Michael, Kitty, Colin, Jason, Adam, Tom and Mike, and Neil

A Rose Pink Production

IN CONSIDERATION OF

CATS

a collection of observational drawings, poems and

notes, A to Z, from the writing desk on the joy and

wonder of cats

Introduction: I am Cat that I am. I am that Cat not. I, mere biped as I am, curl upon the carpet like a would-be cat and peer into another kingdom, the successful principality of fascinating fur and free-roaming former gods –

Felis Catus. I hold cat conversations with these animals on all fours and record my observations that stretch back over Ten Thousand years of human association. From this state of fascination I relay my thoughts and feline feelings to the world of words, but truly it is beyond all words this silent state of cat rapture that I try to capture. It is a place of play, rest and essential nature that intersperses with the focus of stillness. The temporary residency that they permit me the honour to experience is a blessing. To spend time with cats is to spend time exploring the natural relationship between our own personality, soul and spirit. In Vietnamese culture, cats have been honoured by being given one of the yearly signs of the Zodiac replacing the lucky sign of the Chinese Rabbit.

Not being overly interested in words, 'our cats' allow me a little creature comfort of belonging, a little time to be at one with them. Our particular cast of cats from which I draw my observations are: Dinah, Hector, Iolaus and Willow (British Shorthairs – pedigrees and accidental moggies). Yet all of my former encounters and associations with the Cat Kingdom arise to inform me. Cats are free of human stresses and have laid back, patient personalities – there is no rush with them. Enjoyment is always to be found and had in the 'Now' of time, which they occupy with commensurate ease. In their 'Oneness' and unified approach they lead by example and allow me the forgiveness of my split thoughts.

In their domestication, cats love contact – physical, emotional and mental. Yet they are 'Moonrakers' by heart, clandestine gatherers that group together in swinging clans, clusters and clowders. The cats all put on their Midnight Mitts to escape at night and know where to get their Kitten Kicks when needs be. Amassing in a kind kindle of cats at the end of the garden, they know all the backstreet's Hot Spots and local, trendy Jazz Joints to frequent. They often come in late at night swinging their tails and singing,

"Oh, a rinky tinky tinky."

Our cats like the fast, string-plucking 'Flea Music' of the banjo and ukulele whilst not being over fond of playing host to a swarm of blood suckers, particularly not the trio – Fleasome! They also like the wild, sombre, soulful fiddling of the Gypsy Cat Kings mixed in with the big double bass sound of Reverb & The Wandering O'Malley Alley Cats. Though birds beware, they have it in for the Early Morning Warblers practicing their arpeggios!

Their favourite cabaret act is the famous escapologist Cheshire Cat and his Juggling Chainsaws, who always manages to escape from imminent beheading or being cut in half by sharp implements. Their least favourite act is the wildly irreverent, subversive Performing Mouse with clogs on from Old Amsterdam. They think it is the wrong kind of showing off and his follow-up "wacca wacca" comedy tells them home truths and shortcomings they do not wish to hear. Comedy for the heckling and killing, indeed!

Depending on the cats' moods, drunken soliloquies of bygone tales by Puss and his Blasted Boots propping up the bar can be mildly entertaining or a thespian bore. I think it is a generational thing, but they seem to prefer Garfield. Either way, the cats like the fast-talking, mischievous kind of role models best. They dislike the pooch, but like the hooch – the more illicit the better! Yet they do not like drunk, obnoxious or sarcastic cats or those with too many penchants.

At dawn or dusk, conditions are either right or wrong for successful hunting when the cats become low, slow, silent Hunters slinking their way forward toward a frozen moment in time. Then they stop, hunch and coil their back haunches before springing and pouncing. Every nerve is attuned and focused in a single would be murderous Act-of-Death. Birds, mice and leaves are legitimate prey. In between these Hunting Times and Killing Sprees they occupy themselves with cleanliness, independent learning and the assorted Ten-Thousand-of-Cat-Things. On a cultural note, their favourite Art Museum is, of course, the National Paw-trait Gallery.

If cats have time on their paws and can be bothered, they like to follow you around. They like company, and if you do something unusual they will come and investigate. If I re-arrange the furniture, for example, or tidy up the amassing, encroaching general clutter they will have a quick shufti. If I sit half way up the stairs (which is the favoured place I, and nephews of theatre frogs, like to sit), they will slowly join me. Cats are great comforters and, like so many domestic animals interacting with the human species, are great healers. They offer us soothing warmth and relaxation, as well as presenting us with the many gifts and presents considered by some to be vermin.

Cats are the great commanders of cushions and the royal proclaimers of wisdom, for in their natures they remain essentially untamed – a reminder that all cats are proud to be 'Wild at Heart'. You may approach, but always remember that it must be on their terms. Cats, like lions, are known to lash out if teased or in distress.

However, these occasional acts of ferocity are tempered by personality. Whereas this is most true in our Dinah, huntress and mother, it is least true in our Hector who is quite content in being Unwild. Apart from an occasional ounce of devilry, Hector is totally domesticated and consequently likes everything done for him. Nature and basic instinct are not high on his list of evolutionary qualities whereas creature comfort, laps, cushions, being held and generally adored, are. Hector is naturally tame and is easily offended if you try to resurrect the killer instinct in him.

> "Are you mad?" he says. "I've only just got Humanity trained enough to look after my every whim, need and desire. Why on earth would I want to go back to Jungle Living?"

In his own way Hector is a very clever cat indeed!

On affection and aggression: Our cats like to rub up against each other, and often against humans too. Hector is alpha-male supreme. Iolaus, as beta-male, is learning his uncle's tricks, but when Iolaus displays these newly acquired skills for our attention, Hector will not tolerate it and leaves the room. Hector cannot and will not share attention or affection in this way.

As Iolaus is now more secure in the pride, he knows he can command number one place by ousting Hector in this way. Yet Iolaus understands that it comes at a slight price of occasional aggression from Hector. Iolaus counteracts this by being cheeky and nudging his uncle out of the way to try and diffuse any potential animosity. When this kind of contact is being made, Iolaus walks by Hector's flank and head-butts him sideways hard under the chin.

However, you will often find the boys sitting together in a paw-on-each-others-shoulder, uncle/nephew embrace (which is considered by some as being a tiny bit gay!). This is not usually a problem as they will rest there together, and even sleep in that pose in a warm cuddle of affection. Yet once in a while full-scale war of cat fury breaks out. If Hector is not in the mood he will forcefully glare at Iolaus whose tail begins to whip agitatedly in response. If Iolaus does not back down Hector will pin Iolaus to the floor until he is wailing pitifully in submission.

Affection and aggression are outcomes of the same observable behaviour pattern. They fight for love and attention, a kind of top dog (sorry, top cat) situation, when the reality is there is no need for all the jostling since there is plenty of Love to go around and be shared. Who knows what the score is between them, but somewhere I think they are keeping a tally; cats might forgive, but they never forget.

On the downside, both Hector and Iolaus think it fair game to pick on their respective sisters. We actively discourage this, but have been unable to train the males to stop it. It is one of the few interventionist actions we take to try and curb this particular aggressive behaviour pattern. However, most cats, like old dogs, are not for teaching in this way.

 **On all kinds of cats and their realisation:** Laidback, mellow, vocal, quiet, cuddly, active, demanding, sun loving, nest building, sagacious, generous, affectionate, roamers, fighters, lovers, sprayers, long-haired, short-haired, manes, moulting, trimmed, tummy rubbed with fur like fluff, striped,

spotty, blue, whiskered, tailed and non-tailed, smoky, jokey, aloof like lions, ferocious, brave as tigers, young and old, fat and thin, scrawny, scruffy, paws like mittens, extra clawed, tortoise-shelled, shaded, graded, lightly, sprightly, and oh-so rum-tum-tuggeredly, stretched and balled, tightly curled, yet forever arching, rolling, on their backs, on their fronts, on their sides (right and left), stretching, yawning, meowing, me-me-me-ing, in and out the laundry basket, opening doors, up amongst the books and breakables, hidden in drawers, lost in cellars, on top of wardrobes, balancing precariously on banisters, doors and fences, given to climbing, in-ing and out-ing, usually on four paws, but sometimes on two – all kinds of cats are given to different situations and all are growing up in divine individualisation.

Once worshipped as Gods and controllers of the Afterlife, the self-realisation of cats and their kingdom is coming along splendidly.

Basking

The cats are basking in the sun
(Come, come, everyone
Run and bask within the sun)
The breeze in the leaves is having ever so much fun.

Come here, sit still,
Upon a green sill
That overlooks the world,

A city view
From Primrose Hill
Offers all the joy of a promise heard.

Come make love in the afternoon
On a carpeted floor –
Rolling on rugs we both adore –
And forget the world as we close the door
For the end will come all too soon.

Until then we will entwine,
Drink each other's love like wine,
Feel warm together, yet forever raw.

There is hope in the sudden sun,
Sun to come for everyone
And we pray that there is more

Run, run, the cats are basking in the sun.

On being brushed and groomed: It took a while for the cats to succumb, one by one, to the ritualistic brushing that regularly takes place on a Saturday morning. Interestingly, it seems to go in an observable gender/behaviour pecking order: first Iolaus, then Hector, followed by Dinah then Willow, although this can change depending on the cat's mood. The boys are certainly the easiest to brush. Dinah gradually became accustomed to it. Willow is rarely to be seen when it comes to brushing and grooming by human hand. If she ever is in the mood she indicates it by quietly waiting on one of her favourite spots: lying on the footstool or the stairway landing, curling up on top of the laundry basket or on the bathroom mat.

As grooming is a submissive action – a surrendering of their will to a higher will – it takes some cats more time to trust than others. So, on a Saturday morning, I put aside an hour and place a Kate or Joni album on the CD player, bring out the blue rubber zoom-groom brush and hi-tech Fur-minator, and place newspaper upon the rugs to collect the different types of shedding fur – down, awn and guard.

To keep the waiting cats amused I pull out the scratching post with the helpless toy-dog sacrifice tied to the top of it, left over from the previous Friday night's strange Wiccan ceremony. They hold secret clan-meetings that we occasionally stumble upon; such arcane, pagan and cabbalistic practices result in sacrificed mouse heads and bird bones being strewn across the floor or effigies of dogs brutally treated.

If we hide, staying silent and out-of-sight, it is sometimes possible for us to observe the midnight rituals of a coven of cats, which is always interesting – a kind of homebrew Hammer Horror. A menacing spider the size of a child's hand balances on top of the scarred, sacred scratching totem post. Feathers, toy dogs and mice are all part of inanimate, but legitimate, target practice. The vivisection of soft toys is often involved allowing the reading of entrails, runes and remains.

These Masonic Midnight Meetings are taciturn affairs where the cats converse psychically with only the occasional strange, deep, significant meowing sound to be heard. They communicate through slow blinking and an articulate tilting and turning of the head. Woe betide anything that crosses their scalping warpath or stumbles into their covert coven of Occult Templar Cats.

However, I digress.

Iolaus is the best at the grooming game – perhaps the most ready to be submissive and succumb to pleasure. Because of this willingness, he sometimes has to hang around to the end, whilst I attempt to entice and capture the less willing. Iolaus has a problem here. Even though he loves this game, his fur is rather thin and consequently cannot take too much brushing otherwise he develops a little bald patch between his shoulder blades. Yet here is a time when Iolaus is far from being Hopeless or Useless and is just the best-behaved cat of the lot.

Hector can enjoy being groomed, but can be a bit grumpy if too firmly handled or if he is not in the mood. He will not let his tummy be brushed and likes to play with the fur as it accumulates into a huge ball. Dinah will now actively seek out a brushing whereas before she, like Willow now, would not be touched. A multi-coloured ball of fluff and fur, the size of a rat, is the result of such grooming which Hector likes to pounce upon, attack, bite and kick – it is an easy target and unmoving prey! He also likes to chew the fur and paper kitchen towels, whilst Willow, if present, prefers to scratch, rip and shred anything she can get her claws into.

The cats soon disperse as, after the hour/album is up, I bring out the dreaded machine hated by most domestic animals: The Hoover. As I sweep clean the rugs of unwanted, accumulated cat hair, the cats disappear or take refuge at a distance and glower at the moving, whining machine.

Hector is bravest and tries to hold his own (I think it is part of Hector's smart-laziness, as he does not usually want to shift too far from his favourite chair. As he wants to be the first back in it, he does not like to lose too much ground to the sneaky others). For a while, after the hubbub of the Hoover, suspicion creeps in, but within the week the cats will find their grateful way back to the strange, grooming ritual of brushing, scratching post and paper towels. It is, after all, focused attention and pampering, and we all occasionally like that.

On cat's eyes: Some cats have green eyes, some blue, or smoky grey, or brown, or many mixed shades inbetween. Dinah and Hector have eyes the colour of champagne; eyes that seem to dilate a million times over when necessary. Then, at night, they reflect red, small circles of colour and deep wells of pitch black like orbs of living darkness. Sometimes their eyes can be impressive slits or hypnotic startling circles. Hector has the most perfect rounds of eyes that make him look like a night owl. Iolaus has brown eyes with slight inner circles of green whereas Willow has smoky green eyes – like their rogue Peckham fathers!

Cats are slow to blink, once every few minutes as necessary. Lying down in front of them and looking up into their eyes, the energies reach out to you from the Other Side. Receiving regular Darshan and cat compassion in this way makes the world suddenly feel warm, bright and connected. Cats' eyes are reflective and enable us to be contemplative as well.

Cats can also communicate in cat winks, but this takes steady practice to observe and understand. Their eyes are designed to have a Hunter's edge, but they have poor close up vision, which is where their whiskers come into play – sensing and receiving motion information to send to the brain. They love the Twilight, but not the total dark.

Cats' eyes respond to the different stresses and challenges of their situation. Wide eyes (dilated pupils) can express fear, excitement or playfulness. When Hector's eyes grow wide you know he is about to go wild with some kind of insane cat game. If the pupils become constricted, they might be feeling threatened or are signalling aggression. Cats' eyes should be clear and moist. They also have a protective, third eye lid/membrane, which is usually not visible, but can be a useful indicator of sickness if your cat becomes unwell. As far as cats are concerned, eyes are for staring, glaring, ignoring and closing. Oh, and for looking as handsome and pretty as possible.

<u>Cat-herd</u>

I have become
A lap for cats.

Got myself a pocketful of purrs –
My strumming fingers run through creatures of fur

All for the luxury and the love of it.

The cream of the land is given and I accept

In Cat Heaven we all can rub and lick
And slake our thirst.

I have become a solitary, contented cat-herd!

*

On cleanliness: Cats are clean creatures, fastidious in
their fur-licking rituals with their exquisite pink and
raspy tongues. Thus they maintain a daily cleansing
schedule and routine that is a prerequisite of

functional self-love, of looking after self and those in your family/social group.

For them, this can consist of personal hygiene or the washing of others. Often their grooming will take on a social significance; whether together, in pairs or in a group, they all convene to share in this cleaning ritual. When grooming in this manner, they nip and bite into their paws and remove any flaking, rough or shedding sheaths from their claws – essential for use in defence, climbing and hunting.

Cats lick their paws to wash their own faces and eyes and reach behind their ears. They like to keep their coats meticulously smooth and clean. Often the cats will sit on the floor and lift their legs at an acute angle in a mad, fur-cleansing frenzy (beware the ensuing wheezing, fur ball cough, particularly of the longer-haired cat!).

Only on occasion, usually when washing each other between the ears, will the cleaning activity lead to nipping, biting (particularly of the throat and neck) and pinning down of their neighbour on a larger, more riotous scale. Hector, who particularly likes to show his dominance over Dinah, usually initiates this. Sometimes, he needs to be actively discouraged in this activity, but Dinah is more than capable of handling Hector's bullying.

Often we will find the cats huddled in pairs, one paw over the other cat's shoulder, licking and cleaning their neighbours ears, neck and head – all the areas that are impossible to reach on themselves. During this cleaning ritual they show their satisfaction by emitting different affable meows and purrs.

Giving into grooming pleasure (particularly Hector), they completely submit to the contentment of partaking – singular enjoyment of the shared cat state. In their rejoicing of surrendering to this inclination, a job of work and gratification, they give their greatest and most perfect thanks. A lesson to grumbling me indeed when having to compete with others for the bathroom sink and mirror, or when tidying up the mess of others!

On comedy and being comical: Comically quizzical are kittens and cats with their love for everyday stuff (blankets, boxes, wine corks, curtains, laces, lids, paper, pens, socks and shoes, threads, wardrobes, wool et al). With perfect timing they can be in-and-out of things, are totally unselfconscious, and are very good at enjoying the moment.

However, if they are not quite so good at laughing at themselves, they are very amusing for everyone else to watch. They just cannot help their curiosity. They are like a team of Keatons and Chaplins with their crazy cat antics – a fantastic riotous comedy club. We still wake up every morning to find dragged socks and underwear in incongruous places around the house. Likewise, cats at Christmas can be bauble breaking, tinsel eating, tree knocking rascals! Stockings, ribbons and oodles of wrapping paper are certainly some of their favourite things.

Sometimes cats like to hide, just for fun, under a blanket or duvet, inside a box or large paper bag. They climb in (or under) and hide, peering out with wide innocent eyes. The others like to jump upon, play with or scratch out the one hiding. Then ensues a game of 'cat had' where they chase each other and tear around the room before scarpering up the stairs. These are all set routines and outcomes usually descend into moments of comedy violence and slapstick. Like all youngsters, it fulfils a need for speed and thrills.

Sometimes they just like to lay either side of a slightly open door and tap underneath through the gap to tease each other. Whether their more riotous play is for fun or a build up into a frenzied release of nervous hunt-kill energy I am never quite sure, but there is never a dull moment with our feline friends. They are our "reasons to be cheerful: 1, 2, 3, 4…"

On communication and the language of cats: Cat communication is sophisticated, combining verbal and non-verbal elements, and yet has a simplicity of expression which is pure, delightful and direct. Cats are known to twitch, lick (paws, lips, human fingers and hands), bite, nip, dab, claw, flatten (ears, tail and body), arch, stretch, blink, stare blankly, glare silently, gaze upwardly, slink, knead, pad, pull, wag, agitatedly whip (tails, that is), jump, flip, turn and roll over, sit up, curl round, freeze, hunch, lower, launch, hurl, head-butt, nudge and nuzzle.

This, and very much more, not only happens singularly but also in complex combinations of varying behaviour patterns. Whatever it means, it is all part of essential communication in the Kingdom of Cats that we humans are left to amuse ourselves with and guess at. Likewise, with the positions of their whiskers, whether forward, up and out or lying flat against their faces, they all have their different intricate physical, emotional and intellectual meanings. They also have a spiritual aura and mysticism surrounding them and you never know who, by association, is linked into their consciousness from the Other Side.

The language and speech of cats is equally vast. Vocally they can meow, miaow or mew, purr, wildly spit and hiss, scream, chatter, chirrup, brrrp, brr-eow, sneeze, greet, grunt, growl, trill and sigh. All this adds up to a huge range of animal emotion, vocabulary and communication. They certainly know hunger, fear, aggression, threat, as well as knowing how to warn of danger, show anger and become as focused as Diana the Huntress when the need for safety in issues of territory and motherhood arise.

Cats know how to express happiness, contentment and relaxation. From minor irritation (slight twitching of the tail), through slow relaxed, luxuriating blinking, to full on fight and fright in the rising of hackles, hissing and swishing of tails, they know how to communicate to each other and to us.

In Fights of Flying Fur, full investigation is given but if you poke and accuse a cat they are most likely to poke and accuse you back. That, or just ignore you and walk away. The predatory growl, the chirping and chattering when observing out of reach bird-prey, are sounds of threat, excitement and frustration. I am sure that Dinah even tries to replicate bird-like sounds, but then she is a chirpy bird herself and the most communicative of our cats.

By observing and listening to our human vocal interactions with babies, children and each other, cats have learnt to extend their vocabulary to attract our attention and thus stand more of a chance to get what they want. A short grunt can mean hello, but there are different types of greetings and associated rubbings. Long repetitive meows can mean that they want something and 'Why are you withholding it?' This is usually associated with food and feeding time or with wanting to be picked up.

It can mean that you have not spent long enough stroking and petting the cat in question. Other cats will then curl around your legs; head butting and rubbing your ankles whilst miaowing up at you, individually requesting your attention as well. Cats can be quite demanding at times. Three short meows means 'Stop that I have had enough' or 'Excuse me I need some more'. This can relate to picking up, scratching under the ear, stroking under the chin, etc.

Short, hard meows often mean they are complaining. Hector is expert at this type of communication, particularly if you have just removed him from his favourite chair. Sometimes you have to modify your interpretation of cat by checking the wag and agitation of their tails and adjust your general gist accordingly.

Lots of little chirps usually mean they are talking to you in a convivial, conversational way, expressing their generally happy dispositions and jovial natures. This often happens if they are nearby and you call them by name or they want to find you for some company and a bit of a cat gossip catch-up! Dinah will do this when I have come in from the shops. Whilst I am busy unpacking the grocery bags she likes to cat natter and I, in return, tell her about my day.

Deeper, en masse, repetitious meows mean that I have been neglectful and that I am being rightly chastised. This usually happens when I have been locked away for too long on my own, engrossed in writing, and that sunsets and sunrises have collided once more. The cats remind me that it is time for their feeding and a cup of tea for me.

Prolonged whining and wailing (best demonstrated by Hector and Iolaus) means the cats are lost, lonely, stuck or demanding of attention. However, they often do this if you close a door and lock yourself in a room occupied with something/somebody else. They want in on the action, so this din can go on outside the door for upwards of half an hour, which is very annoying. Like a baby's cry, the sound the cats make is very disturbing on the ears and you have to give in.

Little grunts can mean 'Please continue with your pleasurable stroking' or, if emitted in their sleep, mean that they are far away dreaming of catching mice and birds in the satisfying world of cat dreams. The pleasurable purr can take place after love-making, in mothers feeding their kittens whilst whispering their love, or in the tonal buzzing of the satisfied cat sitting on your lap sounding like a baby's rattle or a distant outboard motor on a boat chugging away.

Like Shakespearian actors, all of the above vocal meanings can be altered by the projected length, pace, pitch and tone of the utterance. Some cats recite excellent soliloquies on the roof at night but, on the whole, they are not the greatest of singers even though they like to treat us to the occasional, cacophonous choral practice.

Most cats are rising to the communication challenge and are willing to learn the art and joy of dialogue with humankind (although they do find us a bit slow on the cat language uptake). Dinah definitely understands that we communicate through a series of vocal pitches and sounds and has increased her range in response to being around us. She is such an intelligent girl.

However, I might be wrong in all of this, of course, taking the zoologist and reader on one of my poetic journeys of wonder and delightful nonsense. It might just be that we humans like talking out loud. Often it is easiest to project these translations onto those who do not really understand, but are around when others are out of the house. What conversations with cats have we all held in our moments of solitude and aloneness? They in turn have humoured and indulged us for they, like us, crave a crust of company, familiarity and hopefully an occasional little snack of protein-based food. Dinah has even taken to eating different types of cheese with me for morning Elevenses. What will the mice think of that?

With all this observable behaviour of cat culture going on around me, who knows what learning and lessons in love the next steps of our entwined evolutionary journeys might take. Cats are great role models; they know how to have fun, are very alert to danger, which makes them play safely, but are adventurous, independent, freethinking, free-willed and very high-spirited. Cats seldom have accidents (although the unfortunate few do get caught up in desperate escapes and run-ins with cars to the heart-break of owners).

Coming home to a cat is a great comfort for many people, particularly those who live on their own. Being a Cat-herd is not easy and some women/cat ladies have taken their feminine instinct for cat caring and cat company too far. These 'cat women' might need professional help and some of their cats need spaying or neutering.

Like humans, population increase in the Cat World at this point is not necessary or desirable. It is estimated (and estimates vary) that one non-spayed female mother and her offspring can be accountable for producing over 400,000+ kittens in a seven-year cycle. Responsible ownership and education is definitely required in this area.

On curiosity and new things: Cats are curious creatures and enjoy, however tentatively at first, investigating new things in and about the house. Even whilst viewing something new suspiciously, they will sniff and tap until, on greater inspection, they are sure of what it is and what it does. Then they treat it with their usual indifference unless it can add to their greater good. Except for Hector, that is, who walks boldly into every situation. He is the most curious of cats and is the most fearless when it comes to the inspecting and cross-examination of things. It also might, in some round about way, involve more attention for him.

Cellars, attics, and open windows leading to roofs and next door's house all interest Hector; stair cupboards, large drawers and wicker baskets too. Willow will sometimes follow him, as she likes to be clued in to what is happening about the joint. Iolaus is the most nervy and scared of all our cats and will baulk from most things, particularly if you are carrying laundry or a large object in your arms or when you are folding bed-sheets, shaking out quilts, etc. Dinah is sensibly tentative and enquiring but is usually nowhere to be seen, as she is less interested in this kind of event – the introduction and exploration of new things. In her dignified growing age she prefers not to be disturbed.

On cussing: When required, cats can curse and cuss worse than us humans. Rarely, and mostly borne out of jealousy and of a territorial unwillingness to share, they will strike out at fellow cats and sometimes even at the hand that feeds them. Hieroglyphics of the worse kind come spinning out of their furious mouths, fizzing and spitting like fireworks. If they are tormented or teased, scared or annoyed, they will scratch deeply, swearing and biting like Wild Cats.

If unsure or uncertain of a situation, the cats will circle slowly, Paw by Silent Padding Paw, tentative as to the Long Arm of the Law that might suddenly grab them. One leg in front of the other they chirrup and chirp like a disturbed bird at the subject/object of their distress. For example, if an unwanted cat arrives on our cats' turf, it is usual for the alpha male cat to slowly herd them off the property and out of the clan's territory. In Hector's case this takes a while as:

1) He has to be found by the other cats as he is never around when they need him ("Clever or what?" says Hector the Shrewd.)

2) He usually has to be woken up and then be alerted to the current danger ("Who needs more 'lerts?" asks Hector the Wise.)

3) He has to be directed towards the intruding alien and shown their whereabouts ("What danger, where?" inquires Hector the Disinterested.)

As a rather slow, lazy, yet cleverly dim-witted cat (no flies on him), Hector is disinclined to this type of fronting-up and removal activity. He only does what is required, and then very begrudgingly, because the other cats gang up on him and push him into it (as alpha male they know it is his job, duty and right – no flies on them either!).

Surprisingly, Dinah can really hiss and spit and has the widest ranging blue-fury vocabulary of them all. Because of her easy going nature and having the most complicated relationship role, Dinah is the one most likely to be put in distress. The others often pick on her, so she needs a colourful lexicon to choose from. Under duress, Hector has a tendency to baa and bleat whereas Iolaus brays and Willow gives out little cries.

On damage and previous distress: Putting kittens/cats through early distress or ill treatment damages future relationships. Torturing or teasing teaches them the wrongness of touch and trust, which in turn can lead to mistaking aggression for affection (and vice-versa). Being allowed to enter a cat's personal space is an honour – and given their delicate and sensitive natures, they need to develop trust and love to be part of the wider interaction between the human and other kingdoms. They do not respond well to the control or imposition of another's will, as they are hugely resourceful and independent. So, depending on the level of the cat's confidence, it is important to show respect by listening to and observing their individual needs and responses, as each cat needs to be approached in a unique way.

No cat likes to be cornered and they will re-coil and run if they feel trapped. It is the thing they dread the most, and they will do anything they can in legitimate slash-and-claw techniques to escape. Cats need space, and will feel hounded if you try to restrict them in any way. Traumatised kittens and some rescue cats find it very hard to share their space and might become very territorial and vicious towards each other. Cats imprint and remember such things, which can cause them to mistrust and avoid certain people for a very long time, if not forever. Cats have powerful memories for this kind of unwarranted mistreatment.

On detachment: Often considered aloof, cats are keen observers and can focus on both the inner subtle planes as well as the outer realities. They can sit, watch and stare for hours either sitting upright at the window looking out onto the passing world, or kneeling, front legs folded back in on themselves, in a kind of restful prayer position. From these positions they can reflect on the subtle in-between spaces, levels and dimensions of the spiritual kingdoms as well as the many ways of the world.

Often cats will experiment by partially closing their eyes to aid their attunement. They change the degree of eye-openness to help adjust their brain waves to the inner realms of meditative beauty whilst still remaining anchored in the physical world. They are acutely aware of surrounding sound, but can zone it out. In Zen like repose, still and absorbed, they make good examples of how to maintain the daily meditational practice of detachment. They show us self-composure and serenity.

On Dinah: Dinah is named after Alice's cat in Wonderland – aka Satin Mist Silver Moonlight. She is our Molly Mother and gentle Aquarian Queen given to the understanding of Humanity. She takes everything in her stride. Dinah is a beautiful, shiny, silver tabby with the smallest, flattest, cutest nose and largest almond eyes you ever did see. She also has Dusty Springfield dark eyeliner around each eye for added effect. Perhaps Dusty, like Egyptian Queens before her, copied the cats! Some say Kate Moss has cat's eyes, but Dinah is prettier and less harsh in her lines and has a natural legitimacy to wearing fur.

To add to Dinah's perfection she has one wonky whisker and a bent eye lash on the right side of her face. She is the possessor of strong, square shoulders and a permanently fixed grin like the 'Smile-of-Satisfaction' appearing on the Cheshire Cat. She is our good girl with a wonderful nature. She likes sitting in boxes and suitcases, on top of piles of fresh linen and laundry and lounging on the hall landing. She likes the bed (particularly when newly made) and makes regular visits, more often, I think, than us! She also likes sitting under footstools peering out at you through the golden, tassel-fringe, which makes her even more adorable, looking like an Egyptian Queen of old.

Dinah is a splendid, intelligent cat with a wide-ranging vocabulary. She values her independence and does not overly seek attention. Dinah is also the proud possessor of a silent hunting nature. She can move like silk through bamboo when in the garden – so birds better beware. Her strike pattern is perfect and deadly. She is our quiet, easy going, no nonsense one. She likes playing with paper and cloth mice. A long piece of string is another of her favourite things, particularly when placed in a shoe.

Dinah is the most skilful at playing, balancing and catching (and is the best goalie in the cat paper-football-on-the-bed team). Of all our cats, it is Dinah who would survive a return to the wild. She is constantly occupying herself and honing her skills, and we are always learning from her. She improves her dexterity and adds level of complexities to her game playing unlike the other cats. Her conversation is coming along beautifully too.

Dinah is also the most instinctual of our cats, perhaps because of her experience of multiple sexual partners and thrice motherhood. She has an appetite and nose for food, only quality titbits of course, and has a habit (alongside Iolaus) of occasionally scrounging and scavenging for meaty morsels from around the dinner table. Sensibly, she is stomach led.

We have discouraged table climbing in all our cats, but Dinah's sense of smell is very acute and she, more than any of the others, can sniff out tinned tuna, fresh ham, and succulent, fresh chicken at twenty paces. She, like her daughter Willow, is most partial to catnip and will spend ages rubbing her self with the stuff once procured – legally or otherwise! I think she flits late at night across fences and state borders to get her mitts on it; Moonlight by name, Moonshine by nature.

Dinah has a cat's passport to Anywhere. It is an unacknowledged, but mutually understood, policy of complicity so we do not ask and the cats do not tell where they have gained such stolen goods on the Midnight Black Cat Market. Consequently, we will never know, but she seems to have her catnip habit under control.

Dinah was most informative and particular about where, when and with whom she wanted to give birth. Her first time was to come and find me, waking me up from my disco nap by standing on my chest, padding and kneading away, distressfully meowing until her abdominals started contracting, her birth waters broke and we knew the kittens were on their way.

Dinah instinctively knew more than us what to do and so we let Mother Nature take her course. We were more stressed than her. She took six hours to deliver 5 kittens. The last and smallest (and most eerily beautiful with inverted moon-silver and black stripes) was still born with a white, blood starved, umbilical cord and sac. Named Silver Angel Buddha, we buried the kitten under a rose bush with a candle.

Of course, we were upset by the loss, but Dinah just pushed the dead aside and attended to the needs of the living; food, warmth and life first for her surviving newly born. Thus Henry-Tudor, Iolaus, Mu-Mu and Phoenix entered the world – strong Taurean boys all.

Dinah's second litter arrived whilst we were away in Rome one weekend and a dear friend had the (un) fortunate, slightly distressing honour of housesitting and kitten delivery. He left the house to come back a few hours later to find a whole draw full of kittens; another five and this time all alive and kicking. Thus the Aquarian born Spartacus, Roma, Hero, Yumi, and Brutus entered the world. No mess, no fuss, just motherhood in action for the second time.

The third and final time we were around to look on and help. We soon found ourselves the proud owners of an assortment of six adorable, but definitely hyperactive, kittens (this time Cancerian born). Magic was first and largest, a huge tortoiseshell of a kitten with an extra claw on each foot; Willow at half the size was the runt of the litter. Lola, Gus and Samson plus the Unnamed One were the middle ones. Lola is now a mother herself, making Dinah a grand-dame.

Dinah was perceived as being the most independent and most standoffish of our cats until Willow arrived. Now coming into her 5th year Dinah is mellowing and adopting a more friendly and serene composure that will allow prolonged head, ear and eyebrow massage and even occasional tummy rubbing.

Dinah was rather reticent when it came to purring, the exception, of course, being after ferocious love making with any Tom, Dick or Harry she had attracted and picked on. Dinah has a secret sexual weapon. At night the underside of her tail becomes a fluorescent silver plume and can be seen at fifty cat paces. This attracts a lot of attention even though sexually she seems to stick to the salt of the earth working class! After lovemaking she lies for hours rubbing against the floor purring and purring in an astonishing exhibitionist display of ecstasy.

As the only mother and non-Virgin cat in the house, Dinah has taken to strange ways. Linked to mysticism and meditation, she will come and find me in the morning darkness just before the Sun rises. This visit usually takes place between 5am and 6am when

Dinah calls to me to wake up, meditate and feed her (not necessarily in that order). With her silver, misty aura, and her golden half closing eyes, she holds our total focus until she becomes a channel as breath-taking a tribute to the beauty of Buddha and Mother Mary giving birth to the consciousness of monks and nuns in early morning thankfulness.

After having awoken me with her almost bird-like trills and calls by the side of the bed or even in my ear, Dinah will stand on my stomach and slowly begin to pad her front paws climbing up until she is sitting on my chest. Then she begins to voice her muted purr. Sometimes she will stay there for up to 20 minutes at a time – the only close contact that we usually have these days.

Being a less perfect channel, I am not always best pleased with being awoken so early. After falling out of bed to attend to her, the other cats and my range of morning chores, I look up at the Sun's Dawning and consider the calling of cats mingling with the cawing of crows a marvellous awakening (although some days I wish I could just return to bed).

Dinah is an element of recognised beauty at the start of the day; part responsibility and duty of care, part ever-growing joy and appreciation. After feeding, the cats slink away down the side of the house toward the garden or hunt down their favourite hiding place inside, depending on the will of their mood, the weather and the emerging fun activity of the day.

Dinah never goes too far if it is cold. Usually she just sits outside the door waiting to come back inside to the heat and comfort of the house. After having three litters so early on, she has done her bit for motherhood and having showed us the nature of The Cat Way she is entitled to rest up and settle down into the easy life – not that the other cats will always leave her alone to do so!

Dinah's other hour of deep need for human contact and affection she holds off until the end of the day when she comes and finds us on the bed to say good-night, padding and chirruping away until the light goes off and she hunts down one of her favourite places to rest for the night – usually the un-occupied sofa or on top of the warm TV box.

Dinah was such a tiny thing as a kitten and first-time mother, but she has now become a thick set mum, strong, fiercely intelligent, yet sensible, whilst realising herd independence. I do not think she has a fault, but some say that she is a little aloof as she rarely allows you to pick her up or hold her these days, but that is not my experience of her. On the whole, Dinah just likes to keep herself to herself, whilst enjoying the occasional soccer play and individual attention when it suits her.

Ordinarily, Dinah sensibly sits on the outskirts of us, just out of reach, a perfectly positioned 1 arm and 1 hands length away. Unlike Hector, she is not a lap cat. The only exception is when she follows and sits near whoever has become recently identified as her primary feeder. Her favourite things are being stroked slowly across the eyebrows and being scratched behind the ears. This, Dinah will allow you to do for a very long time. If she really trusts you she will even turn upside down for an occasional tummy rub.

However, approach Dinah too quickly or sharply, or try and hold her against her will, then she will kick against you and bolt as fast as she can to get away. She does not like abruptness or rudeness and will not tolerate her liberty being infringed; captivity in that way is not good for humans or cats. Quite rightly, you will be deeply scratched as a result.

Dinah And The Birds

Pretty sings

The birds are beautiful
In the branches
Swinging their wings, doing their dances,

Tails up, tails down,
A step and a hop,

If I were Dinah I would eat the lot!

*

On distress, pain and disapproval: Cats are very aware and wary of each other in distress. If there is a closed door between them, they will pace alongside it, sniffing and clawing the under edge, trying to reach and re-assure the other cat. They are aware of each other's pain and distress, but if the cause of the smell is too clinical (i.e. one has recently returned from the Vet), the others might even hiss and turn upon the injured/ill cat. Cats do not like change or strangeness and smell is all important to cats. Cats tend to avoid and quarantine other sick or strangely acting cats and will slink off and retreat into a quiet corner on their own if feeling unwell themselves.

Each cat responds differently when being placed in the basket that takes them on the strange and noisy journey to the Vets. Dinah becomes so quiet and submissive it is unnerving. Hector meows plaintively. Iolaus and Willow huddle together. However, once there, Hector is the most easily handled, he even purrs when it comes to needles and vaccination time. After all, it is still all about him and what could be better than that!

Dinah is quick-witted and if she sees an open door, shelf, fridge, etc. to bolt through or hide in, she is off like a shot. Iolaus handles the situation in his stride as long as you are there to comfort him. Willow is subdued by the whole experience and looks up at us in a lost, painful way as if to say, "Why? Please never do that to me again."

It is very rare that we have to tell the cats off and we only intervene if there is a rather spiteful looking spat going on. Then they are suitably admonished. They grumble for a while, and then slink away to sulk. Cats are worse than dogs for learning new ways, as they are more wilful and independent.

However, cats are very good at letting you know when their boundaries have been crossed – they are not looking for love in the same way as dogs. Vocally, they will let you know their disapproval (like infants) in a high-pitched, ear-shattering way. Politely asking them to stop does not usually work. Barking at them ("BOG OFF!") sometimes works, but can make matters worse. Indoors, sometimes a light spray of water from the plant mister bottle is required to disperse unwanted antics. Outdoors, the hose usually sends out widespread panic in the same manner The Hoover does indoors. But these are only ever used to scatter any cat gang warfare getting out of hand.

Usually cats will vanish quickly from the scene of a crime (broken vase, crashing books, fish flapping on the floor scooped from bowls on the mantle shelf, etc.). They are good at scarpering and once gone remain so for a considerable time (or at least until next feeding time comes around). No butter on their paws! Trying to regain a cat's attention once it has gone is nigh on impossible.

Unlike dogs, cats are not good at focusing on, or doing, two things at once. The only exception is to employ the use of certain multiple, feathery, dangly play things when you can try and coax them back into the room again. Unless, that is, they know you are trying to stuff them in a pet-med box or a carry case heading for the Vets. No chance.

Oh, cats know all right! They are canny like that and can be tricky. Your first go at stuffing-the-cat-in-the-box trick has to succeed; otherwise it is 'hunt the hissing cat all over the house' time – everyone's least favourite distress game. You remain unforgiven for weeks, months, even years, as cats can hold you in their memory as 'Most Wanted' in the ensuing Grudge War of crimes against Cat-manity!

On Hector: Hector was named after a dream I had about the positive masculine principle. As well as honouring the wonderful Greek prince hero, Hector represented the opposite of Hecate and the dark side of the Moon – aka Satin Mist Ebony Star or His Highness. Hector (the undeniable King of Cats) is a cat of the most miraculous, happy and luxurious kind.

Although Hector is a jib, and suffers from the hormones and alpha male dominance problems of a neutered would be Tom, he is an Aquarian King and consequently very regal. He is a big, black, owl of a cat with a beautiful, cold, wet, dark-as-coal, symmetrical nose. Blacker than Salem, he possesses a bat-like face when he puts on his wild, disagreeable look with his ears pinned back.

However, Hector is a Posh Puss, a Hector Puss, and our handsome Hector-Hound. He is the perfect cabaret 'Chat Noir'; the King of Puddings Cat; a Blunder Puss and a Splodge Cat all rolled into one.

Hector is a butch boy, a 'look-at-me-and-adore-me' kind of cat, and occasionally, just occasionally, an adorably dumb knucklehead. When Hector poses, he tends to lie nonchalantly (although of course he is carefully arranged) on cushions (usually red, russet and deep orange – he is very colour aware) left scattered on the brown leather chairs. Positioned such, he looks for the entire world like an advert for a magazine: the perfect pin-up cover for Gentleman's Cat's Quarterly. He is very photogenic and is the least likely of all the cats to be startled or flustered by anything. Hector is not a cat to be unsettled and, as a consequence, seems rather brave, braver than he actually is.

Hector is always 'first' and 'foremost' in his mind, and in his consideration and carriage of himself. Subsequently, he is regarded in this manner by others operating in the Cat and Human worlds about him.

He does not subscribe to the notion that you are me (we are each other), nor to the idea that by doing good deeds towards others he shall be mutually rewarded with like. No, he does all things plainly and simply for himself.

Hector has huge attention needs and therefore puts himself centre stage in his universe. At times he is just a big baby by nature wanting to be picked up, put over your shoulder, patted, and soothed. He both needs and wants to be held. Other than that, he is straight forward, simple and uncomplicated, not the kind of cat to be much bothered by anything. He is very laid back and if he were human might be an occasional Stoner, good natured and mainly kind.

Dedicated to the pleasure principle, Hector has a luxurious black velvet coat and large round champagne coloured eyes that sometimes glow orange. His purr is like beaten, melting butter mixed with sugar. Every night he comes to recharge our heart batteries with the power of positive purr that can make good the unwanted and unhealthy reversed small electro-magnetic polarities that have built up in our own human systems. He lives constantly in the relaxed alpha energy wave state. Being in his company relieves our stress. Hector = confidence and happiness. He has an uncomplicated, hassle-free cat wisdom, which means he is complete in all the essential requirements of Earth living. That is why he makes it all look so easy. A flash bastard, but a Saviour of our Universe!

Hector has several favourite tricks, one of which includes reaching up into baskets and bins then toppling them over. He crawls inside to discover what suitable scraps he can fish out and starts playing with the findings (usually bits of thrown away scrunched up paper, discarded pens, rubber bands) whilst scattering the rest of the detritus and rubbish all around the room.

Hector also has a habit of plonking himself down in the middle of doorways so you are left manoeuvring around him. Trying to pick your way over or around him is no good as he just looks at you and gives one single 'brre-ow' and you are left having to give him the much overdue attention that he requires.

We suspect Hector of being the Midnight Sock Monster. At night whilst we are sleeping, one of the cats removes pairs of socks from the cupboard drawer and drags them into the bedroom or hallway. The highest sock count to date has been 10 pairs. It is slightly alarming to awake to find items of clothing scattered around the bedroom and not know who put them there. What on earth have the cats been up to?

Apart from having too much time on their devilish paws, perhaps they think the socks are mice and are offering us strewn presents and strange offerings. Perhaps it is some kind of cat competition combining kleptomania with the card concentration game 'Pairs' only this one is played in the dark with items of clothing? Or perhaps it is simply good fun being mischievous and playing with our morning minds?

Sleeping through it all, we shall never know. On several occasions we have lined them up for interrogation, but when questioned they all look undeniably innocent, supremely so, and continue to wash, look bored, then wander off. Cats are sleek and, like all expert thieves, burglars, and Usual Suspects, have mastered and perfected the crafty art of 'getting away with high jinks and murder'. It is not the doing of it, but the being caught. Even then, they are not that bothered.

"What us?" "Nah, you must be kidding." "No Way!" "Excuse me? Please don't insult my intelligence!" "If you want me, I'll be outside."

All these rebuffs, denials and deceptions can be heard being muttered. Yet it is the kind of mischief Hector would get up to. As he has recently taken to stealing and carrying buttons around in his mouth, we are pretty sure it is he.

However, the most wondrously annoying/amusing thing Hector does (depending on your mood) is to select dark spaces and then sit there. He is as stealthy as the notorious Black Shadow. As he slowly closes his eyes he becomes totally invisible. Whether he is sitting on a pile of dark clothes or sitting on the black, marble kitchen worktop he completely disappears into the surrounding darkness. He does it slowly and deliberately so you can marvel at his magic.

This miracle of camouflage and invisibility leads to your memory loss. For a while you forget all about him until, that is, you sit or stand on him or he startles you by rearing up and blinking. It is a large-eyed blink as innocent as an owl or a disbelieving angel which scares the 'B'Jesus' out of you. Then he meows at you in a particularly aggrieved manner.

"Did you forget me?" he laments in a way that is most ruinous to your nerves and you are beside yourself until all attention is focused back on him.

Hector is clever like that and rather innocently manipulative. He knows exactly how to centre everyone's attention on him with his roguish good looks and plaintive mewing. Hector will get himself stuck in places that his stupidity, laziness and want of attention will not let him get out of, so you have to go on a search and rescue mission. ("I only go missing so you can set up an expedition and have an adventure," he explains). This has even meant Midnight Cat Liberation on our behalves to rescue him from empty construction properties along the street.

Another irritating thing Hector occasionally does is to jump up on the bed when you are tucked up tight still fast asleep, usually at dawn feeding time, then bite and scratch your hands or feet. This usually results in a shout and a sliding kick, a less than delicate thud and an annoyed grumbling and meowing from both sides of the duvet. Disgruntled swear words rumble like thunder in the distance from both cat and human alike. No one enjoys being outdone in our household.

Hector is a very social cat and likes groups of people (more attention, more stroking hands, more rubbing fingers, more laps to sit on, more admiring exclamations of "how very beautiful and black a cat he is!"). He was in his element when the TV crew came to film for the day, all Victorian coming-and-goings on – everybody cherished him. Hector likes to play, loves to climb, but above all other things, he likes to lie on his back with his paws in the air and just be. Sometimes eyes are open, sometimes eyes are closed – it depends on the best effect he can have on those around. Hector has, without doubt, perfected the at-ease, luxury, sunbathing cat posture. It is impossible to pass him without rubbing his belly just like a Laughing Buddha.

Hector loves to be held, petted, scratched, rubbed, picked up and folded in your arms (he is a large, heavy, yet liquid, like cat). If you are sitting for a prolonged time watching TV, you can place a great big, plumped-up cushion on your legs and call him over for his luxury, all over, head and body massage – preferably Thai style. This can last for an inordinate amount of time and you tire long before he does as he absorbs attention like a sponge.

Likewise, Hector enjoys stories, particularly those involving cats and bears, when he is being petted in bed at the end of the day. However, Hector's favourite story is the one about the White Mouse Emperor and the Fat Rat King (he is actually called the Black Rat King, but Hector will have none of it). Even though Hector sometimes has to join forces with the former to overcome the fiendish plans of the latter, it is an uneasy alliance. Hector particularly dislikes the Fat Rat King's tone when he mutters his favourite cat insult,

"Super-catty-ratty-licious-fishy-halitosis!"

The stories must be short, taking no longer than five minutes to tell; otherwise Hector's attention drifts. They need to be to the point, full of adventure and err on the side of the victorious cat in the end. Then, quite story-satisfied, he will slink and find a quiet place to sleep for the night. He has his favourite chair, but more often than not he will sleep right by our bedside in order to protect us from marauding mice, rakish rats and any unsettling sidewinding snakes that pass in the night.

Interestingly enough, Hector is the most healing of our cats – for even in crises he will come to you regardless of your emotional state and sit on your chest and purr. Just purr and purr and purr. He takes on a sympathetic healing role when you are ill and even adopts some of your symptoms (much to our Vet's bill cost!).

Hector is such a magnificent cat (in all his weight and glory) that he is impossible to ignore. By diverting your attention and re-engaging with the Healing Rays of Hector, no negative human emotional state can survive for long. He is the enforcer of 'eliminating the negative, accentuating the positive' and enables the appreciation of life (him) and the acceptance of him (life) through simple purr pleasure. It is his truth of joy after a near-death-experience he had when he was very young. What a Shamanic cat he is.

Hector is so far removed from the depressed, hurt and angry states we humans often find ourselves in, that we are both moved and healed by him. That is one of the reasons why everyone loves him, and indulges and shares in his sense of majesty. Seven heavenly hurrahs for Hector! He is adorable and needs, like angels, adoration back. When your heart is full of Hector nothing else really matters. The world and its problems slowly dissolve away.

Hector likes to walk all over or sit on the Tarot cards when they are laid out in Gypsy Readings. He is ever so helpful like that. As his coat is the colour of jet, he crosses our paths and palms with oodles of good Black Cat Luck. Throw in a horse-shoe and some wild heather, what more could you ask for in terms of

Lady Fortune and Prosperity Charm. Hector, of course, does not care about such things. He just wants to turn your attention away from what ever you were doing onto him.

Hector likes lying on his side on shiny wooden floors and being swirled around in endless circles. He is also fond of water that can be found in plumbing and sinks. He was the first to discover that fresh water comes from out of both the bathroom and kitchen taps and will only drink the cleanest, coldest water – a trick that Iolaus and Willow have now both learnt, but only Hector commands such regular, tap-turning servitude from us.

Hector is not at all afraid and welcomes investigations into cellars, attics, and chimneys as well as cupboard and wardrobe spaces. Once he did get locked in a cupboard for a whole day and, understandably, he howled the house down. As he is so black he is often found covered in dust and cobwebs from such expeditions and does nothing but purr whilst you clean him up.

Aesthetically, Hector is the most handsome of cats. The lines on his head and face are strong, square and beautiful. He has the most amazing muzzle. He likes to sit on any piece of paper that you are writing on or trying to use, and loves playing with pens (that is, anything that is distracting you away from him). Hector is more important than your small, outwardly directed daily concerns. He 'plumps' himself down and that, my friend, is that – an immovable force of Black Cat loveliness.

Hector likes to sit on plastic bags, lie collapsed on arms of sofas and chairs as though reclining on a sunny tree branch, and climb into cardboard boxes and onto suitcases. He will even manage to scale the tops of doors, wardrobes and cupboards if the feeling takes him, although how he finds the strength, coordination and agility is beyond our general comprehension. Hector also enjoys getting stuck (usually between the trellis and the big vine in the garden). He is good at going up and even better at getting you to get him down.

Unlike most cats, Hector prefers dry food to wet. He has learnt how to fetch on demand when playing with bits of paper. Yet he is also the only cat in the house you can throw a piece of paper at and he will watch it fly pass by with total disinterest. The more you fuss and try to play, the more disdain he pours onto you. His will is immovable in such matters.

Once ensconced in your arms, Hector can stay there for an awfully long time (usually for more time than you have and can hold him for as he his heavy). He believes in himself and forces acceptance and appreciation of him onto you regardless of the importance of your activity.

Indeed, I have come to think that there is a Law of Hector in operation that states that the importance of your task is inversely proportional to the Love required for a handsome Hector Puss at any given moment. May we be blessed with his presence for a very long time, because he is undoubtedly the most perfect of cats in all cat kind. He is everything a familiar should be, a healing black shadow that follows you around the house.

Shh! Now, with all that said Hector does have a few faults, which is why we have to whisper. His primary ones are discussed in the observation on Iolaus – jealousy and an inability to share. His other fault is that he can sometimes be a bit grumpy. Like all of us, he has his days of wanting, demanding, and of not being satisfied where he grumbles and meows discontentedly, being out of sorts This particularly happens when he is unceremoniously kicked out of his favourite chair (which he sometimes has to reluctantly share with us humans, the rogue Iolaus and, on rare occasions, the lovely Willow). How very human of Hector to show us his other side. He must love and trust us very much indeed!

However, Hector has one further annoying habit that he has taken to recently. In his need for attention, he circles your ankles and then reaches up to your thigh (he stands quite tall as a cat). Next he digs his claws into your upper leg, gives into gravity, stretches and just hangs there – either mistaking you for a scratching post or expressing annoyance that you have taken so long to show him any attention.

Depending on the thickness of your attire, his claws hurt and sometimes he draws blood. A gasp, a glare and a forceful "no" are then usually heard echoing around the house. Yet this does not stop the Hector Hound, who only wants to be picked up, held, chucked under the chin, and have his head stroked and his belly rubbed. Through all of this he will purr loudly, but pleasantly, into your ear. Who can resist such charms? He is soon back in your arms purring and making you smile.

<u>Hector</u>

Hector's a cat,
A black, fat cat,

The biggest, blackest, fattest cat
In all the flat.

"Hello Hector.
Oh! Hector,
Hello…ooow!"

His claws are sharp,
But he's not so smart

Yet never-a-cleverer-cat-was-seen
For he is the cat from the cat
Who-has-just-got-the-cream.

Hector's as black
As a Shadow Unseen,

Midnight fastidious,
Unkempt, but clean.

He is the loveliest-fat-fattiest-cat-cattiest-
Bat-battiest-black-mat-cat you have ever not seen!

*

On Iolaus: Iolaus was the second born of Dinah's all boy first litter. He is a Lovely Likeable Lad. If I were still a pitchfork stable boy I would choose him to be by my side as my rat-catching companion. Named after Hercules' blond sidekick and shield bearer, Iolaus is a handsome brown tabby and our golden stripy tiger boy. He would always come when called, but loved to roam the big outdoors. He would look good in travelling boots and a hat with a feather.

Although Iolaus's coat had beautiful markings, his fur is thin and the least waterproof of all the cats. Thus, when wet, he looks most like a drowned rat! However, even though Iolaus grew from a timid kitten into a more confident cat and settled into himself a bit more, he always retained a nervous disposition. Yet a steadfast reliability slowly emerged from him and he developed an ability to relax and purr for all cat kind once he could get some attention.

Iolaus is a large, strong cat, taller in the hindquarters than most, but a bit leaner than Hector and Dinah. He is rather slow, plodding and methodical in his manner (which is why he was subsequently nicknamed Hopeless and Useless). Iolaus is the most likely to be startled by anything new, loud, quick, unexpected, etc. He likes all kinds of food, wet and dry, and scavenges like Dinah at the table, although he is often unable to distinguish the quality of what he scoffs and eats.

Iolaus is a greedy boy and consequently is given to eating slightly too fast and being sick. He is the one most likely to go behind your back, picking up discarded ribs and chicken bones from the bins and leaving them strewn around the dining room floor. Iolaus can prise saucepan lids from off plates when he smells fish. He will even snatch the ham from out your hands or sandwich if you are not looking. He is a sneak thief and fast with food. It is a clever, crafty trait, but very infuriating.

When Iolaus was older and more confident, he deliberately vied with Hector for singular attention. This forced Hector, as alpha male, into the jaws of jealousy, which meant Hector had to withdraw from the room and disappear for a while. Hector, being far too grand to compete for attention, is unable to share in that way. Iolaus knows how to capitalize on this and can rid the room of a Hector in mere moments thus eliminating any male competition.

Iolaus has a cute habit of sitting very upright and will, with a slightly open mouth, stick out his very pink tongue. He is slightly taller, longer and thinner in the body than the other cats, so when he takes this pose he looks strangely like my March Hare statue – bold and beautiful, yet slightly mad and ridiculous, all at the same time. When Iolaus sits next to the statue they are strikingly similar (with the exception of the ears), and both share the same gold-bronze coloured coating.

One night, Iolaus was sitting with the March Hare and I as we Moon-gazed out of the window. It was that moment which inspired the poem on Iolaus. He so looked like the March Hare when the notion of the 'Rotating Rabbits' within the Moon came to mind. I thought it would be fun if there were three circling cats instead of rabbits, linked by the same two ears. It was a mad, Moon gazing, lunar, triskele Hare-Cat kind of thing. It all became a bit Gaulish! (so to speak).

<u>Iolaus – Moon-Cat</u>

O great Cat-catch-scratcher
Got myself a cat rat-catcher
Madder than the Mad-Hat's Hatter

O golden Tiger-boy!

Caught up in the rounded square
Of the 3-ringed boxing Moon-Cat's Hare.

Like tea, let Love and Light flow everywhere,
Yet the dormouse slept and never ever dared.

Blessed be the cake in Magdalena's care.

Iolaus likes to pull himself across the floor with his claws in the carpet whilst lying on his side and kicking out his back legs. Sometimes he lies on his back, upside down, and pulls himself along the underside of sofas or up and down the carpeted stairs. Then it becomes a game of stroking his golden tummy hair whilst he is rubbing and scratching his back. He is a good boy and will fall asleep in the crook of my arm.

Iolaus was late in learning to purr, but having spent individual time with him, he became a relaxed cat with an up-and-running outboard motor of a purr; a veritable rattle-bag. He is one of the more vocal and talkative of our cats. Unfortunately, he did not inherit the rich tonal quality of Dinah so his cat-speak was rather squeaky with a grating, monotonous whine.

Like a baby, Iolaus learnt to use this to great effect as his continuous moaning means he quickly gets your attention and you will do anything to get him to shut up and stop. Iolaus will sometimes come and curl up and keep me company when I am locked away writing, but only if he felt totally safe. This means I have to be quiet, not move and focus my attention on my writing (i.e. not fidget), which can sometimes be hard for me, but his company is a good way of disciplining myself.

On looking at and ignoring people: Here cats are in their element. Cats are Kings and Queens when it comes to disregarding you, or me, or anyone else for that matter! They are just as good as Bette Davis and Joan Crawford. Sometimes they might stare at you sideways – mostly when they want you to run about for them whilst playing a game or if they wish to dismiss you from their presence. You are the 'Weakest Link' – goodbye!

Usually cats only look head on at you when they want something: on demand feeding, attention, picking up, etc. Mainly they just lie there, paws outstretched royally, watching you go by as though invisible, unimportant, or totally dispensable. It is nothing personal and usually depends on their mood, but it is a reminder that it is they, and not we humans, who are at the centre of their Turning World.

Cats can look grumpy and mean too, particularly if they start to flatten their ears. Sometimes they will look askance at me when I am trying to distract them from their stare-glare meanness to one another. At other times cats will stand to attention with their two front, petite, neat feet placed together. Sitting upright in perfect Egyptian poise and style, they tuck their tails around their sides and curve the tip to slot in between their front legs. Like this, cats look consummately regal and serene as if they could do no possible wrong (and certainly nothing that you could get irate with them about, whatever your suspicions).

Cats are very good at disdain and excellent in the art of ignoring. Yet sometimes on entering a room, all four cats will turn to stare at you fixedly. In perfect unison they will look at you and you are suddenly caught in an out-take of the Village of the Cat Damned where they are secretly probing beyond your mind into your soul to see if you are a worthy host in the next stage of their evolution.

It is a scary process as the cats turn their Supreme Intelligence away from you to stare away into space and the Big Beyond. Silently, they send back their telepathic report to the Cat Oversoul of your own humble soul's progress. Thus x-rayed, you are left feeling stripped down and unimportant as you creep back out of the room, sorry for having disturbed them, grateful to get away alive from the secret ways of the Cat People.

Unfortunately, reverse psychology does not seem to work on cats in matters of suspicion and allegation. They look at you and say, "Is that reverse psychology you are trying to use on me?"

The only time you can fool a cat is by calling out another cat's name and then they will all rush in as:

1) They do not want to miss out on anything

2) They get jealous of any potential misdirected attention

3) They are curious creatures who want to know what is up and what is going down.

On lovemaking and motherhood: Love making in cats is strangely course, rough, and often painful. Of all the sense and sensibilities of cats, this is not a refined one. It involves the pinning down, the taking, the cursing and caterwauling, the biting, the domination of and over, the sometimes clawing and slashing, the climbing on top of culminating in the final, painful, barbed penetration and screaming. The female then will actively seek out this rough act, replay, endure and enjoy it several times within the given reproductive hours.

Afterwards the female will be as gentle and purring a Pleasure Puss as anyone has ever seen. No call of the mystic here, only the enjoyment of rough earthly pleasures and nubile nights in the giving and taking, taking, taking. Even Queens can become strange sphinxes and minxes when the call of fur, flesh and menses takes them over – a mini-barbarism of rough encounters, rugged enjoyment and endless rubbing against the tiled kitchen floor in cat sexual heaven and ecstasy.

Motherhood ensues quickly after the casual mating of male courtship, though the Toms do not stay around to watch, nurture or help. The female of the Cat species is far too wise and takes singular control over the motherhood process (their instincts and intuitions arising from the single cell of long ago).

Dinah is my only example here for she has been the only sexually active cat of ours. Lovemaking for Dinah is preferably with the roughest and toughest of Toms. She might be a Pedigree Puss, but when it comes to antics in the bedroom department she likes a Sun reader every time! Dinah made a natural mother three times, all nature's mistakes and our Veterinary mis-timings, but oh-so much joy for us and our friends over the coming years.

Dinah became incepted as a mother for the first time one Christmas morning. Being young and it being winter, she was not meant to be in season and we were advised to wait until February to have her neutered. Hector, poor bastard, had already had his testicles removed on the kitchen table (by a Veterinary friend in the late autumn) so was no threat to incestuous fatherhood. Little did we suspect Dinah of having dreams of Winter motherhood, but off she flew and escaped. Come May her first litter arrived.

When the time came, Dinah skilfully employed the same teeth and mouth that could kill so quickly in a way that was so maternal and loving – tender, yet firm. She held and carried her kittens one by one when she wished to move nest and re-locate from the sock drawer to behind the sofa. In her wisdom she re-chose a safe suckling spot and was encouraged to build her new nest for the weeks to come.

How the kittens would whimper and mew in protest whilst being carried on the precarious journey from bedroom to living room. Occasionally Dinah would drop them, particularly as they grew larger and heavier, but she knew what to do from the minute they were born – licking them clean from their mucous sacs until they started visibly breathing and calling out. She ate the first placenta and chewed through the umbilical cords as each arrived. Her natural instinct in action was amazing to see. Clever girl!

Dinah is a grandmother now (not that she knows or particularly cares), making Hector an uncle and great uncle to many a straying niece and nephew. As a mother, Dinah only has to endure and tolerate Iolaus and Willow in her daily sojourns around the house and they all keep pretty good company.

We kept Iolaus and Willow partly because of their unusual beauty, but also to make a foursquare relationship pattern to maximise the amount, type and complexity of roles and connections they could have. Hector makes quite a good Uncle, but would certainly stand no impish nonsense from the skittish world of kittens. He would quash them and their antics with one heavy-handed swipe of his paw if they became too cheeky or took liberties with him (like using him for a climbing frame, for example).

The second time Dinah mated was the evening before the day she was due to go the Vets. Her operation was booked in for the Saturday morning and so, of course, she disappeared that Friday night. She knew all right. The third and final time was due to the fact that we were having the garden fence replaced. So that evening when Dinah got up for her nightly prowl, she saw her opportunity, jumped through the gap in the wall and that was that – disappearing into another garden of nocturnal delight.

Again, Dinah timed it to perfection. Before we could grab hold of her she was laying on the garden floor surrounded by several male admirers all hanging around taking it in turns to have their way. Dinah was obviously busy enjoying the experience whilst genetically deciding on the superior sperm she was busy collecting. We enjoyed the results of Dinah's mating very much: kittens, joy, and deeper understanding of the cat world, our own world of relationships and the inter-play between the two kingdoms. But enough was enough and she was soon under the Vet's control, sensibly being spayed. By then we had run out of friends and homes wanting kittens!

On madness: Cats are sometimes overtaken by a type of lunacy, of running up and down, of calling into the invisible, of throwing themselves against walls and doors, of looking alarmed at the slightest thing, of rising hackles and heckles, and chasing strange shadows only visible to them. This is due, I think, to an excess of energy in their nervous systems and their sensitivity to both sides of the Veil.

So it is that cats sometimes need to go 'mad in the head' and end up playing dab-had with the amiable ghosts and our happy phantom friends to release the build up of invisible electrical energy that underlies all our physical systems. The Moon magnetises this energy and cats express it immediately and in the most direct way possible. Then they forget all about it and put it out of their minds. I wish I could deal so easily with some of my own mental well-being issues and states of sensitivity.

Because of their nervous disposition, cats do not like change and prefer stable environments, fixed routines and regular hours. Even loud sneezes and sudden large or quick movements can alarm the cats and cause wide spread panic, particularly amongst the more scaredy-cats like Iolaus and the younger skittish-kitty, Willow.

Cats will often cartwheel, jump, spin, or run in a mad fashion around the room, or up and down the stairs, for no apparent reason. They might be in fight, flight, fright or just fun, (they might or might not tell you which), but will sometimes career around corners and run full pelt into your legs, sending you and the tea spilling. If they run at you full speed it is like being tilted at in jousting, knocking you off balance and nearly breaking your neck.

"Out the bloody way, pests," I hear being hollered in the hallway as another scampering accident of teenage tearaways and terror is re-enacted. The loveable rogues!

On meditation, peace and stillness: Cats can seemingly stare into space for a very long time before slowly closing their eyes and drifting off somewhere particularly pleasant. Or so it seems to us human observers. Sometimes they will slightly re-open their eyes until they are fully assured of settling into peace and stillness without being disturbed. This is a very good preparation for meditation. They prefer silence for this practice which they do daily. However, like

Market Yogis of old, they can also find silence within the household hubbub if required.

Conversely, at any loud noise or close by distraction they will become alert, hyper-aware and ready for appropriate action. They will run quickly away if startled by sneezes or loud offending machine-made noises, particularly The Hoover or the spinning Washing Machine. There is no hesitation in the recall to the land of the living. No sulking or confusion or asking of questions.

Cats understand the simultaneous nature of the inner and outer states, and know how to operate in both. If disturbed, they will prepare again for 'sitting in stillness' often giving a little sigh – knowing that it is the prolonged, outward breath that supports their pursuit of inner calmness. Sometimes the right paw will extend and touch the left. Sometimes they will bend at the elbows and knees and fold in their paws in genuine feline genuflection.

Apart from their daily prowling between 5am and 7am and 6pm to 8 pm (approximates as stalking is seasonally light adjusted) the cats are often to be found in various poses for reflection throughout the house. They know all the quiet soft spots on which to curl comfortably and where best to avoid the constant human traffic. In this way, cats have perfected the art of complete focus and stillness and hate being disturbed by stompers, noisy feet or human clodhoppers – particularly those who are spatially challenged!

Cats like the smooth for they are by nature silky creatures. They might only choose to slip into silence on occasion, but watching them practice their daily peace is an amazing feat to see. Here they are at home with themselves and the Universe, not doing, just being. They achieve that quite readily and with deep intent and contentment. In such repose, they remind us that they are not just former gods, but formidable creatures of today who have truly stormed the gates of their Soul's Heavenly Kingdom.

Like the plant kingdom, cats have attained a connected spiritual resonance in all three aspects of their bodies: personality, soul and spirit. Dogs make note, for cats will not take kindly to any interruption from this state. Indeed, sitting around doing nothing whilst looking up into the sky and beyond into the invisible is what cats do best. Beware them though, for they are Masters-in-the-Making and know The Cat Way. They do not suffer fools gladly. Better still, try joining them. For if you can manage quietness they will sit by your side or curl up on your lap where you can inwardly join the deep lake stillness they inspire.

Sitting still is not always so easy for us humans, particularly when the kettle calls, and daily demands or the Fidgets start to take over. Yet once you have got out of the way of yourself and your thoughts, sensations, movement and feelings become calmed, you can slip into a wonderful world of reverie and Quiet Water. Riding in on the alpha-wave state, inner Adventures-of-Consciousness begin taking you to the bigger extraordinary 'You' – to the Cosmic place where the spirits of old friends and family reside and where spiritual insights await.

On name knowing and the hating of yellow canaries: Cats know their names, their cat given name, their human name and their own infamous, unfathomable, nom de plumes. Whether they choose to respond or not is another matter entirely. It really depends on whether it suits them; acknowledgement and interaction, as previously stated, is always on their terms.

We know cats recognise their human names because if you call out loudly to them they will come, and if you whisper it softly to them close-up they will purr. Their real cat names are lost to secret, so Sorcerers and Witches can no longer call on them as familiars or press-gang them as reluctant recruits in their ancient Wiccan arts. Cats have been delivered from such bondage since the Mediaeval Dark Ages, but can choose to re-enter service to The Craft if they wish.

Of all the creatures that survive today, only the artful, crafty yellow canary can penetrate into the world of cat names, which upon utterance renders a cat paralysed and powerless. It is the canaries' stunning karate blow equivalent to a Vulcan nerve pinch. This is why cats have placed the killing of yellow canaries on the top of their wish lists just in front of fishing

for trapped, bowled fish (easy prey), the tormenting
of dogs (soft target) and the showing of utter disdain
for those lacking in charm (the right thing to do).

Oops! There goes another goldfish...

I found the cat with a golden grin
And a bowl where a goldfish should have been,
Half a tail and half a fin
Poked out its tight gripped mouth.

'Blasted cat!' I wished to shout,
But Nature is as Nature do
No point making a hullabaloo

For a self-satisfied cat
With a sprat
Somehow catches the mackerel too!

*

On people: Cats are independent, smooth-talking, talented and ambitious social creatures. Consequently, they have inveigled their way into the affections of mass humanity. In return for being fed, watered and groomed, they offer us comedy, affection, exasperation, and comfort – but above all the pleasure of integration with another kingdom.

It is in this shared, crossover space between humans and animals that evolutionary healing and inter-species relations can occur and develop. Cats are not only instinctual, but are also deeply intuitive. They will even sacrifice themselves in order to be heard from beyond the Veil in human dreams and visitations – proof of their survival over death and the fact that animals do have souls!

Most of the time cats do not care what people might think of them. Judiciously, though, they do not tend to bite the hand that feeds them. They might even take to licking that hand as a way of soliciting social interaction and acknowledging trust, but it is mainly because we feed them and show them affection. Very wise creatures indeed to bring out the best in us!

However, cats certainly do not take well to being told off or being considered a disturbance. Shooing a cat away from the computer keyboard or from the paper you are just about to read might lead them to taking umbrage. Cats like to be spoilt and hate to be ignored although they will ignore you for a while whilst they plot some kind of intriguing revenge (usually chewing through a lava lamp wire!).

Cats have very good memories for that kind of thing. They will then return to annoy you in some deliberate, artful way or at the very least trip you up. They have mastered the quick art of ankle unbalancing and can topple a human at twenty paces whilst licking their paws, looking cute and innocently enquiring,

> "Oh dear! Was that me? I'm sure that you're mistaken."

Cats can also glare, stare and glower like nobody's business. Ears flattened, tempers and tails will flash as they spit their animosity toward those who have crossed them. Momentary spates of fight and spite flare up in the battle of cat wills against human interference and determination. The cats do not stay around for long.

"People!" they tut with derision as they dive around another corner or disappear up the stairs.

You can positively hear their scorn, but they will be back. For reasons best known to themselves, they do not like to be gone for too long.

On perfecting the reposes: Cats are here to teach us 'Royal Ease' if we can but learn it. On rest, they are masters. They sleep curled, looking cute with paws wrapped around their muzzles. We are jealous of their relaxed divinity. On waking they yawn, take in extra oxygen and commence their daily stretching routine before moving, ready for fun and exploits.

Cats are always practising the art of relaxation whether on their backs, reclining, curling on their sides, or lying on their bellies with their two front paws stretching out in front, touching in connected prayer. They are keen observers, sitting upright at the window watching the world go by.

Cats are also often busy with the art of reflecting, kneeling in silent intent, eyes closed, whilst meditating upon the World of Wonder. They are laid back often to the point of seeming laziness. Our male cats are definitely the best at looking cool and inviting in this art, whilst our female cats are superior in the refined skills of balance, movement and alert action, being more focused, able, and accomplished than the males.

However, all cats have perfected the art of Yogic Repose and, unlike humans, tend not to confuse or merge the different types, their meaning or their purpose. Sometimes our cats are to be found in a room arranged in precise geometric patterns as though sitting on a grid of invisible ley lines. At other times, they are assembled in perfect symmetrical poses like carved book ends in mirror image of each other on the arm-ends of sofas.

Occasionally three of the cats will curl up together on a chair, one mass of different coloured fur with their heads sticking out at triangular corners like a Pagan priestess of old (all except Dinah who keeps to herself and is more of the independent Buddha nature).

On perfection: A note to all would-be disfigurers of cats believing this will save one more place in Heaven for humanity: this is not so. Cats might have reached perfection before us, but maiming a cat's tail in this way to ensure the possibility of your mean, competitive spirit securing a place in the After Life will only bring you back to the Earthly planes in acts of restitution.

The great Cat Spirit in the Sky will make sure of it, for they do not forget and often bear grudges in the on-going karmic wars between animals and man. Pray they kill you quickly if you should ever come back as a bird or mouse and cross into their prowling territory. More importantly, may your veneration and protection toward the animal kingdom extend and grow in your understanding of Life. By the grace of Mother Nature and God's Super Nature go you and I and all God's creatures great and small.

On playing: Cats are, and like being, both indoor and outdoor creatures (in the Summer our cats live outdoors and build nests of leaves and bark to sleep on). They love to playfully chase the breezes and go where the desires of the day take them. If so wishing, cats can turn anything into a game, which is good as a cat's life is for playing – learning through fun.

Catch, retrieve, pounce, dive, dab, spit, hiss, claw, leap, chase, surprise springing and pinning down, as well as other such activities are all part of their daily enjoyment regime. It not only passes the time, but also keeps the instincts charged and honed. You never know when a return to the feral wild might be necessary – and then such savagery might be the key to successful survival. Unless, that is, they learn to walk on their two hind legs and become skilled in the art of using tin openers. Then they could live forever on the tinned delights of tuna! I put nothing past them.

The cats have already learnt to manipulate handles and open doors and cupboards. Often they are found on kitchen surfaces licking recently used tin openers that have been involved in prising open salmon, tuna, pilchards or ham from cans. They are not encouraged in this habit, nor are they allowed on the dining room table at meal times.

Sometimes the cats' games are comic, but sometimes they are so utterly serious and focused that it reveals their underlying genetic disposition; play becoming a re-directed source of ferocity and hunt-kill instinct. Flies are great ammunition – flying food and fun.

Early Morning Mischief – Cats!

Hector plays the piano.
Dinah's unimpressed.
I shuffle in my pyjamas –
Disheveled early-morning mess.

I open the window

Fast food in the form of a fly
Buzzes in and buzzes by –
Bluebottle Heaven!
Like buses, none then one,
Then three, then seven…

Willow and Iolaus claw at the sky.

Now cats chase and run,
Galloping each and every one.

No cup of tea is safe!
The CD's totter, slide and scatter,
The vases wobble whilst weighted underneath…

The cats inhale, sniff, then sail
Upon the early morning breeze.
They are so eager and so pleased
To play this catching game.

I shout and call out all their names.
They look at me as though they do not care.
I look at them and shout, 'Don't you dare!'

No rhyme or reason in so much fun
Just natural born fly-killers – all for one!

Except for Hector.

"I think I'll go and sit in the sun," says Hector,
"And watch from windows the busy people go by."

I know what he's up to, he's awfully sly.
He'll artfully sit so people can admire and say,

"Oh my! What a beautiful cat."

I know what he's thinking.
I know what he's at.

Next life, next life, next life, please –
O to be a treasured cat!

*

In play, the cats (singularly and collectively) hope for birds, mice, bats, frogs, fish or at least a falling leaf or twig, but it is the humble piece of paper that remains their favourite toy whether to claw, paw, scratch, tear, sit on, rip up, chase or fetch.

Pieces of paper scrunched into balls and hurled across the room turn shiny wooden floors into fashionable cat ice-rinks. The cats slide, fall, slip and collide in a free fall, free-for-all, argy bargee of competitive play as they scramble for the paper puck. If the paper gets trapped down the side of a chair or stuck under the sofa, the cats back up slightly, shuffling their hind legs, wiggle their haunches, then launch themselves onto their paper prey as if there was no tomorrow.

Cats often find it difficult playing together as their individual frolicking distracts the others and they lose focus. They are not so good at sharing in this way. Cats will claw, throw, curl, catch, hit, pounce, leap and jump in pursuit of the paper ball (seen in their eyes as a bird, mouse, fly or spider). They will even stand on two legs unceasingly batting the piece of paper between their two front paws until their teeth sink into it in a frenzied re-enactment of legitimate bird-hunting murder.

Cats are honed, natural born killers training their instinct, whilst making pleasurable games out of their desires and driving impulses. Picking up the paper ball in their mouths they will walk to the nearest shoe and drop it in; then begins another of their favourite games. Rolling onto their sides they will happily spend inordinate amounts of time pawing and flicking the tiny paper ball at the bottom of the shoe with the utmost precision. Their needle sharp claws become like seasoned French pins picking snails from a shell.

Sometimes the cats will freeze like a statue and pretend that the ball of paper is a mouse in a hole. They bide their time staring into the inner dark of the shoe for they know they only have one chance. Then, quicker than lightening, they are scooping the now dead paper ball out on a glistening needlepointed claw. Into their mouth then off they run to slowly slaughter and behead the poor piece of paper under the dining room table and chairs.

Shoelaces and string are equally beloved and intriguing. Other than that, feathers and two cloth mice (preferably infused with catnip) tied to the end of a long piece of string on a stick is their next favourite clawing game. Stalking the succulent spider, swiping the beautiful butterfly, and pouncing upon any unfortunate daddy longlegs that happen to be zooming by follow this. Looking up to find a cat with firmly closed lips, but with the legs of an insect or arachnid sticking out of their mouth still wiggling, is a gruesome sight.

In fact, the only place our cats dislike playing is under blankets, duvets, sheets, etc. which is unusual compared to previous cats who have loved climbing beneath or playing in the comforting warmth. For them, beds are for sleeping upon, not underneath. I think they fear some kind of entrapment. Only on one occasion have I found them going berserk in the bedroom. Half way through changing the bed I was called away, foolishly leaving an old duvet with a few feathers poking through hanging on the wardrobe door. Well, you can imagine…

<u>Cats Ahoy!</u>

The cats are turning into birds.
It is quite absurd!
They slice open the duvet cover
And eider duck down gathers a-feather
All about them.

They cut and splice
And spy for mice –
Extra fur in colder weather.

In the billowing, bellowing bedroom
They buccaneer and mutineer,
Pouncing in puffs of white plume
As they hunt feathers together –

A Pirate-clan of clever bedfellows!

And we have to agree –
Time for a new quilt in our snuggling-in forever.

*

On the football front, Dinah likes playing goalie on the bed and is by far the most skilful of the cats. Quicker, faster, higher and more agile than all of the rest, she can stop, bat, catch and kill any would be ball of paper in its flight. She can even turn complete circles in the air from being hunched down, lying low. Not even Beckham could curve one past her!

Hector is slower, clumsier, but will bring objects back to you so you might continue his favourite game of 'throw and fetch'. (I think he is practicing to be a dog in his next life if the Transmigration of Souls programme will have him! That is why he became known as Hector Hound because he acts so like a dog and will follow you around if called). Iolaus preferred flying feathery things that he could bat, catch, claw and put in his mouth. Willow is not so keen on any of these games.

All the cats like to pursue birds and will chase feathers and things upon the wing to their demise. Claw against breast, teeth upon tender necks and song throats, until the final flurry of death shows the supremacy of the cat's instinctual body at work – a sort of fly-drive-in, fast food chain, murder kind of thing from where the camouflaged cats hide in the leafy garden.

However, play between the cats can sometimes turn serious. Nasty, fur-flying nips and bites, means instinctive hierarchy and preservation are at work with one cat lying on their side clawing up at the other one who is slowly circling ready to pounce, bite or claw. Alarming hissing sounds and deep throated caterwauling means war is escalating, but this is rare and only to be expected within any contained group. We all have to work through the pressure-cooker of discontent when so many are involved in social living and playing together. A cat's motto:

> "You can't always get your own way or get away with it, but it's always worth trying."

On precision: Our female cats are by far the best in this department. However, as Hector and Iolaus are sitting opposite, glaring at me, they do not know why I am bothering to mention such things. They consider it to be an audacity on my behalf. Now they are both ganging up on me, grumbling slowly away by my side so I think I shall try a different approach… *(see 'On stumbling/falling/missing')*… and continue on to the next heading.

On purpose: Cats, like all animals, are divine expressions of energy of the Monad, the Great Evolving Godhead. They give great pleasure in evolving relationships in both their kingdom and in ours as well as intruding into the realms of the bee, bird, butterfly, dog, fish, fly, frog, mouse, snake and spider (as well as the neighbour's garden!). Cats know their purpose and do it with singular intent.

It is a fact that you cannot distract a cat from its singular attraction. They can sit for hours in front of a mouse hole without moving. Of the several things they like to chase, they know what they are seeking and are remarkably particular. Cats like to be in on the action. They live independent and group lives, learning how to establish relations based on social interaction and territories. They have firm boundaries.

Cats are highly independent, often secretive and can act strangely as though on a whim. They have investigative natures (based on curiosity) and preferred choices (based on discernment), which are powered by their own tenacity and free will. Have you ever tried telling a cat to do something? They are just not interested and will ignore you or think you are insane.

Cats like to be fascinated and engaged and will keep you on your toes at the top of your game. They are inquisitive and they in turn fascinate us. Of course, the opposite is also true in that they are equally content in doing a whole heap of nothing, just sitting around and being quite disinterested. Cats, unlike dogs, do not get frustrated or bored and do not mind appearing dull.

"What do you think I am?" says Dinah in an offish manner. "Entertainment!"

Cats are generous, open and giving creatures, but can be guarded, particularly when drinking water. Wisely, they remember that drinking from a watering hole is a potentially vulnerable place where predators of old can take advantage. Their night vision developed, like owls, into the excellent hunting of the dawn-dusk mouse and creature feast. Yet they are willing to deliver these 'gifts' to your door and give them up for a preferred, easier meal out of a tin or packet (or preferably some fresh fish or meat you have just cooked for yourself).

Cats are happy operating at either end of any given activity spectrum as the two distinct opposites, frenzied hyperactivity and stillness, sit easily within their natures. As kittens they love comedy, but become statelier as they grow. Crazy individual and group antics can often be heard on stairs, in hallways and seen dashing around in gardens as they flash their tales to caution in their endless scampering and scarpering. They are, quite frankly,

"Superbe!" (French accent).

On seeking you out: Food, warmth and affection – we all need those – but cats choose their companionship accordingly. Unlike dogs, they are particular and, like the weather, subject to vagaries and indecipherable moods. When cats want attention they will come and ask. They come to push, nudge or head-butt your hand or chin until you are ready to abandon the task at hand and stroke them with undivided attention.

If a cat has specifically sought you out then they will not leave you alone until you have satisfied their desire. This is particularly true if you are the proud possessor of a cat like Hector who will simply sit on your hand if you are still writing or using the computer's mouse in any vain attempt to accomplish something other than the coddling of him.

What becomes interesting is who they are specifically targeting for their affection and why. Similarly, it is always fascinating that different cats will come to say hello to specific visitors popping in. It is probably some kind of 'invisible vibe' thing, but it certainly is curious and not always an immediately obvious connection.

Sometimes the cats will gather around at my feet, seeking out spots in the sun of the half-shuttered living room, or the shade of the bedroom, for companionship in an afternoon's moment of shared, sleepy siesta. My eyes close as I fall into a doze and they will all lie around me, slowly curling up tight, one watchful eye still half open, in case I move or disturb them, safely just out of fingers' reach. They are just waiting for assured stillness before they themselves succumb to sleep and the sharing of a human bed, sofa or sun drenched piece of carpet. How lucky I am to steal such moments with them in an otherwise hectic modern world and busy living situation!

On self-love and sacrifice: Watching Dinah with her third litter I came to observe more closely her response to motherhood and her interaction with the kittens. Often they would be feeding or demanding to be fed, when she would get up suddenly with no notice or warning, walk to the food and water bowls, feed, wash, survey the surrounding environment with keen intelligence, and then re-group herself and the kittens as appropriate. This, she told me, was right relations for, in putting herself first in moments like these, she was centred in self-love. From this correctly aligned point of balance and fullness, others' needs could be met without the 'compassion fatigue' or 'over protective caring' we human sometimes find ourselves caught up in.

When the kittens were playing with the older and bigger cats Dinah, as watchful mother, would sit and monitor the situation. She would only ever intervene if things got out of hand. She would let the kittens take their knocks and paw scuffing where necessary, but would quickly go on the offensive to defend them if the older/bigger cats became mean and tormented the kittens too much.

A firm paw cuffed too hard from Hector could knock a kitten flying across the floor whilst Iolaus could growl and clout like anything if the kittens got too close or clambered all over him. Dinah showed us in her concerned observation and keen actions the balance between 'protection blanket' and the taking of the 'rougher, experience medicine' that sometimes is part of the School of Life.

Whilst the kittens were still feeding on her milk, Dinah would lick their bottoms and milky stools so nothing was wasted. This, I am told by my Vet friend, also helps stimulate the kittens' excretory functions. At other times of feeding (going onto soft solids) Dinah would call to the assortment of kittens hiding, sleeping, and playing all over the house to the kitchen in a very particular way. Having fed a little for herself she would then oversee the tiny feeding frenzy.

This, Dinah informed me, was a sacrificing of her needs for the good of the group – to ensure all had some nourishment and were learning how to feed for themselves. Only after all the kittens had eaten would Dinah return to eat any remaining left over titbits. This was her Love in Action, balancing the needs of others and her self. This push and pull towards the kittens was also a way of her dealing with the imminent loss of her offspring, which soon came.

One by one they were taken. After they had all departed, Dinah would roam around the house meowing in pursuit of the lost kittens until an acceptance of the change, of all that she had prepared them and herself for, became a reality. They were gone and she was alone. Dinah only cried for a little while – a despairing mother's lament and wail – until she fell into quiet and an understanding of separation.

Dinah knew then that the bonds had been broken. Just like she had eaten through the umbilical cord at birth, this was her signalling that the emotional/astral cords had been cut and her sons and daughters were free to live their own independent lives. What a great gift! If only we humans could be so conscious of the right timing involved in cutting the ties that bind we would all be living healthier lives.

So that quiet, which was inevitable, descended upon the house and within it a new acceptance was found. In that aloneness Dinah experienced a deepening change, a new sense of happiness and settled into her more mature self. Dinah, like so many of our fine, four legged friends, but more than most, is a remarkable cat indeed.

On sleep: Cats make excellent Sleepy Heads and have undoubtedly mastered the art of sleeping.

(Sleeping is when most of us humans are truly connected to the spiritual state, which is a shame in being so divinely unconscious, but can lead to some fantastic dreams).

Cats understand the need for much sleep, which is good as it is during the sleep state that they are in contact with their Spirit-Selves, as well as allowing their own inner biological growth, repair and homeostatic healing to take place. Like us, their Spirit-Self never left the harmonious Bliss State (the firmament of Heaven), which is busy beaming and dreaming us alive on this side of the Veil.

Unlike most of us (and by that I mean me and mine), cats have regular lifestyle patterns that are healthy for general living and well-being. Other than grooming, feeding and watering, they are often found somewhere between rest and sleep before the dynamic, active states of explore, play, hunt and kill take over and focus their outward everyday attention into some kind of orderly activity. Cats know how to Power Nap and can sleep at any time, but also know when to wake up and tell us the time of day.

On smelling and sniffing: This is important in the cat kingdom for smell is prioritised in the hierarchy of senses. It is a wonderful inter-communication thing. You see it in operation in every cat during his or her daily routine even though we do not share the exact sensitivity toward the power of sniff. It is vitally important in the first few moments of birth, as kittens are born both blind and deaf. They must instinctually sniff out their mother's belly and teats. This warmth, affection, connection, sense of snuggling and belonging, and primary sustenance, is something they, like us, remain in pursuit of for the rest of their lives. This can also include a sense of competition for food and survival against their siblings and other cats if necessary. That is why squabbling and rivalry between kittens is useful in teaching Life's Tug-of-War fair/unfair game.

So food, warmth and affection become the first qualities these Ancient Gods seek in the arc of life from birth to death… and very admirable qualities to be in pursuit of they are. Laws good enough for these Gods are good enough for our household too. Their preferred smell is definitely fish (tuna, salmon or anchovy) followed by chicken and ham.

Dinah will play with green olives, pawing, rolling and licking them, but all of the cats go mad for olives stuffed with anchovy (even those covered in garlic and chilli if you are a Willow-cat!). Bleach can also strangely attract, (is it the ammonia of urine they smell?) and if I have been swimming, my chlorine soaked hands often get a good sniffing and friendly licking which is nice, but odd. Perhaps it is some kind of cat high?

When first gathering together in the morning in the bathroom, the cat clan usually meet and greet one another with a sniff. This snuffling occurs at both ends — one at cold, moist nose end and either one long sniff and a push up against the tail end, or two or three quick sniffs at the rear. This sniffing procedure of the nose and tail end not only checks identity (that they are who they say they are and are not imposters, clones, nor have they been inhabited overnight by intruding poltergeists), but also gives advanced warning of any potential sickness.

On stability and change: Cats value security and stability very much. In the main they do not like change. This has actually become an observable 'generational' trait – as Dinah is the most easily put out by anything new (e.g. situation, person, or unwanted object) and is the most cautious, whilst Willow (the youngest) takes new things in her stride; no questioning, no sniffing, just straight to acceptance as bold as you go, entrusting it into her world. She looks quizzically at us asking,

"What's the fuss?"

After that, Willow disappears and ignores it (whomever or whatever it might be) whilst the other cats remain wary. Yet, whether accepted or ignored, changing circumstances or new things fundamentally do not bother Willow, whereas with Dinah and Iolaus they can visibly perturb. Hector is more nonchalant anyway. As a rather laid back cat, he genuinely is not bothered by the shifting landscape of any new occurrence or situation. That is because he is not the most aware of cats and knows that ignorance can be bliss.

However, out of all the possible scenarios of change, house moves are particularly traumatic for cats (we have put ours through three so far). What starts out as a chore for us and a fun game for cats (extra paper, plastic and bubble wrap to play with, more packing boxes to jump in and out of) ends in harrowing upheaval and howling. Once, poor Iolaus refused to come and had to stay over night on his own at the old flat until he was picked up the next morning.

Meanwhile, Hector was strolling around the new house looking for all the world that he had been there several years and was busy exploring, hiding and generally being in command. Dinah and Willow were deeply distressed. Willow hid in the tiniest unreachable space behind the toilet in the bathroom for hours. Dinah did not know where to hide in all the noise and confusion, did not know where to eat or where the litter tray was. Most unlike her to have an accident in that way, but we made it all right for her as she was so obviously confused and distressed.

When Iolaus arrived the next day he looked so scared and startled that he bolted straight away into Willow's favoured hiding place and ousted her. By now, though, Willow was willing to go on a walking tour with her Uncle Hector, exploring the many rooms of the new house and chasing the breezes up the chimneys. Strange the ability, adaptability and willingness to change of certain cats and not others, and the different time it takes them to feel safe. It took us a few days to quieten them down.

Being a Leo (fixed fire) myself, I also like stability and constancy so I know how traumatising it was at the time. Now it is all a distant memory and they love roaming the wilds of the new, big, old house and having space from one another, whilst still being able to gather for social occasions in any one of the many rooms at their disposal.

Initially, they loved to gather in the blue room, which was their holding room on arrival. It later became their favourite room as it was the quietest, but they have all been unceremoniously thrown out of it now it has become a working therapy room. They did not thank us for that and, in revenge, will sit and howl outside the door if they know we have company.

On stroking and clawing: Cats might allow you to stroke or pet them often. Some insist on it and will even wake you up in the middle of the night with a head butt to the chin (Hector), a faint purring in your ear at dawn (Dinah), or a horrible, whining, complaining meow (Iolaus) at any time of day if he is hungry. Willow has her own secret ritual. Of course, they mainly try it on with us softies!

Sometimes, rather annoyingly, the cats will skirt your fingertips a hair's breadth away out of reach – cats know how to hold their vicinity proximity to the advantage of their own individual comfort and safety. Generally our cats like to be held (their choice), but they must be put down straight away if they want to get down. Holding a cat against its will is against the Cat Law of Freedom and will soon result in them clawing or kicking against you.

Most cats enjoy their heads, necks and ears being scratched and chucked, sometimes under their chin and along their jaw too. You should always start stroking in these areas, as this is where they lick and groom each other so, in one sense, they are expecting contact. Hector will also allow you to gently lengthen, massage and passively stretch all his muscles as well as articulate his joints and stimulate his reflex points.

Sometimes the cats will lie brazenly on their backs inviting a 'tummy rub', but beware! This is a potentially very vulnerable position and place for them, so if you do attempt this manoeuvre you must start very gently and must monitor the flicking of their tails. If the tails get too agitated, it will lead to a short, sharp bite, a clawing, or even a prolonged curl-up and thrusting with the back legs like a kicking rabbit. Once your hand is entrapped in a cat's ferocious, curling wrap, the only chance to extract your fingers and hand without further scarring is to freeze and hope they will let you go without further ado (no chance with Willow who takes no prisoners).

This is when you need some kind of external distraction (preferably a noise from somewhere close by) so that you can retract the fragile flesh of your fingers and hand from their perilous, biting teeth and boxing back-legs and claws. If you cannot retrieve your hand from what started out as a sweet, lovely game of tummy rub, but which has now turned into one of deadly serious self-preservation, you know your skin and veins are about to lose blood. In tooth and scratch against human skin, the law will favour the Long Arm of the Claw every time. In cut, claw and quick dagger action the female of the species is to be most feared.

It is important not to tease cats otherwise their reactions can become wild and their savage, scalping revenge on your fingers and toes whilst you are asleep becomes fair game. Their aggression can be playful, be based on fear and pain or even stem from a feeling of sexual stimulation. However much a clawing hurts, a cat should never be declawed. If cats get spikey or wild, there is usually a good reason. That means both your and their behaviour might need investigating.

However, to find the cats all lying on their backs on the living room carpet, like a little family of sea otters, is a sign of great trust. Rolling from side to side, just flipping for fun in a purrathon of pleasure, is an extraordinary gift; a dazzling display and sharing of their natural affection and hospitality. We must treat those times of intimacy with kindness and respect.

On stumbling/falling/missing: *(also see 'on precision')* Okay, the male cats are, on the whole, the best at this activity. Still all our cats, on missing something (birds, paper etc.) or falling off the mantle shelf, will automatically begin licking their paws and preening themselves as though nothing had ever happened (or been intended to happen, so why even mention it?). It is almost as though they are embarrassed by their failure and suddenly 'click' to another activity as though this had always been their intent. Cats, I believe, dislike being unsuccessful.

Our male cats are clumsier, but they also care less. They sometimes misjudge heights, surfaces or the space/size ratio required to manoeuvre around objects. Everyone in the room quickly sits up on 'fragile alert' when Hector or Iolaus tries to wander around the photographs, flowers and glass vases perched on the piano, mantle shelf or nearby table. Not so with the girls.

Interestingly, Hector is the only cat who walks the ivory keys in the creating of atonal cat music. Like me, his music making is not a natural talent, but he is enthusiastic and getting pretty good in the plonking note noise stakes. Dis-chords for paws indeed!

On suffering: Dinah is our main teacher here – on suffering and how to end it, that is. As she has got older she is unwilling to endure anything she does not like, want or considers disrespectful. Having taken so much flack, she is not the 'whipping boy' for the others and will not be put upon in such a way when the other cats lose their manners.

Dinah gave so much in her early life. From her experience of giving birth and the later responsibility and coordinated sharing she had as a mother, Dinah dedicated herself to the raising of three litters of extra-ordinarily beautiful and characterful kittens. Now she is mature and statelier, Dinah asks for very little except to be left alone and company when she chooses.

However, if Dinah needs something (letting in, letting out, food, company, scratching post, play, brushing, stroking, etc.) she is very clear in her signals and boundaries. In the strength gained from being such a wonderful Mother, Dinah showed us the way to prioritise and re-centre amidst the process of so much change. By vocalising in a simple, firm, unafraid-to-ask way she could relay what she most needed; direct requests to which others could appropriately respond.

Hector, on the other hand, just lives on the pleasure principle and has a different sense of balance. If you do not move from that point of perfect self-love you will be fine because you will not invite suffering in. There is of course the rare occasion when his nose is put out of joint by one of the other cats (usually Iolaus) or by us when his jealousy or inability to share causes him to suffer, but generally Hector is not one for off-centring himself in the first place.

> "Suffering?" Hector wisely asks. "What's that? Why would you choose it?"

He is quite right, of course. The pain game – where is the value in any of that? If only so many of us were not conditioned to it.

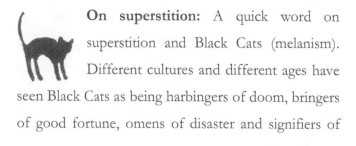 **On superstition:** A quick word on superstition and Black Cats (melanism). Different cultures and different ages have seen Black Cats as being harbingers of doom, bringers of good fortune, omens of disaster and signifiers of

prosperity alike. This is often predicated on whether the cat is walking left or right, or approaching you from the front or from behind. To the Travelling Black Cat it is of course a matter of mere direction and inclination – the tosh of superstition is purely ours!

Folklore establishes Black Cats as familiars of witches (who could share their nine lives), which is why the Puritans were not so keen (more fool them!). Yet the mediaeval mass killing of Satanic Cats only resulted in the rat population increasing – and we all know what happened back then. ("Bubonic or what?" says Hector. Score +1 for Black Cats; -150 million for humans. Good or bad luck? Go figure!). Indeed, melanism might be responsible for aiding the Black Cats immunological pathogen resistance as well as providing effective camouflage for ambushing prey.

Likewise, whilst cats might occasionally take our breath away by their antics and beauty, they do not suck the breath from babies. Cats, on the whole, do not always like babies and children. Too much noise, fast, erratic movement, and competition for their liking. Similarly, any myths surrounding Siamese Cats (Moon Diamonds) need to be dispelled. With their blue eyes (pale, whitish, light blue through to royal and navy blue), they are clever, lively and keen cats not mean or spiteful creatures as sometimes depicted in movies.

From monarchs and gods to witches and warlocks, from brides and pirates to gamblers and anarchists, from fisherman's wives and men at sea to the Chat Noir cabaret and inspired writers, the appreciation and reviling of the Black Cat marches on unabated the World over. The final word goes, of course, to Hector our own black cat and that word is – "Supreme". Of course, he would say that, but he might well be right.

> "Oh, by the way Hector, did you know that there is a National Black Cat Appreciation Day?"

> "I was not aware, but I am glad that there is. Does that mean I get an extra treat?" enquires Hector.

> "No, you're appreciated every day."

"Just asking!" he retorts. "You humans *are* funny!"

On water: Cats, on the whole, do not like water, rivers or rain (the rare exception being the Turkish Van, originally living by the lakeside, and the Bengal, which is naturally athletic). You never see them with an umbrella for that is what trees, shrubs and houses are for – waterproof protection. Yet cats have a highly developed spiritual trait that mirrors one aspect of the nature of water. Like a still pond, they have developed an extra-ordinary Tranquillity of the Senses. This is particularly evident when they are in repose and reflection. In this regard, cats can be supremely serene. Yet, like the rolling, splashing waves in the shallows, they also know how to frolic and have fun scampering back and forth in eternal delight. This is what gives them character.

Cats also like what water can bring – fish, particularly of the trapped, gold variety in bowls and ponds – and what it can attract (i.e. birds to a plentiful rain-filled bird bath). They like fresh running water to drink and play with, but do not like showers, although we did once own a Siamese cat called Suki who enjoyed walking around the bath and did not mind getting a little bit wet.

Generally, a wet cat looks disgruntled, unhappy and vengeful. Unlike dogs, soggy and bedraggled pusses are a rather pathetic sight for sore eyes! The demeaning expression 'drowned rat' comes to mind. This, of course, is particularly insulting when aimed at cats. Whereas wet dogs just playfully shake and forget, cats seem to ever-remember and never forgive the drenching humiliation until they can suitably turn the tide.

On Willow: Willow is a silver stripped and spotty tabby who is as quick and slippery to catch as a salmon. Her head and neck have black and silver-grey stripes, whilst the rest of her body is daubed with dark grey-silver spots. Her tail is perfectly lemur ringed. She has a small, pretty face, round eyes finger-smudged with green and lots of long whiskers that stand out (which makes her look as cute as that favourite things song in the lovely Sound of Music).

As the runt of Dinah's third and final litter, Willow was the smallest and most delicate of them all; the sweetest little kitten you ever did see. Sometimes she would even curl up on our chest and fall asleep peacefully in the energy of the heart centre. Willow became a bit more of a scatter-brained, skittish-kitty interested in playing (mainly outdoors given the chance), eating and sleeping lots (like any withdrawn teenager), although as she has grown older she is settling down a bit more.

Willow is definitely one of the e-generation of cats who likes wires, computers, screens, TVs and flickering/moving images that she can sit in front of and tap at with her paw. Willow will chase a ribbon or a ball of wool for a while, but generally she is disinterested in these kinds of games and prefers to roam wild and do her own thing.

Willow would own an iPod if she could and would certainly be good at texting and keeping up-to-date. Her favourite nibbles are poppadoms, salt and vinegar or chilli-flavoured crisps, and crunchy cereal bits left stuck to the side of a breakfast bowl. Unlike the other cats, she does not care much for milk, but tastes can change.

Willow is definitely a Cosmopolitan-reading-girl-about-town-kind-of-cat – very pert, independent and a thoroughly Modern Millie. She keeps herself to herself, thank you very much, so please do not be surprised or offended if she ignores you most of the time. In the World of Cats it us Humans who are the dispensable units. However, she does like smart people like Professors and will come bounding in to greet them!

Willow, like Iolaus, learnt Hector's water trick, but rather than drinking from the tap she tends to wet her paws, wash her face and ears, then lick her mitts clean – more of a daily, dawn, cosmetic, washing routine than anything else. She often sits in the shower tray washing or playing with a small ball of paper or is to be found sleeping in the bathroom sink (she is a Cancerian after all).

Generally, Willow will sleep on random things (jeans, towels, and warm fresh laundry are her favourite), but is most often to be found curled up on the floor in the centre of the soft, Chinese Rose rug in the red room. It is as though she knows that the central, circular pattern was specifically designed as her place to sleep.

Willow likes to sleep tightly curled in a ball, her head tucked into her two front paws. She is slowly allowing us to handle and brush her more as she is more able to surrender and submit to stroking. Fingers, thumbs and toes are still legitimate targets in her game of play. She likes sitting in boxes and particularly on paper, and when she sits nearby, she is at least two arm's lengths away so she is safe. You have to lean forward to be able to reach her if she wants to allow contact.

As the newest, littlest member of our cat family everything is still very much on Willow's terms – non-negotiable. However, she is a Twice Turner, which means that if she is in the mood and allows you to approach, she will collapse onto her side and then roll over very swiftly a couple of times. She will reward you by meowing once appreciatively and then allow you to chuck under her chin or scratch her ear.

Unfortunately, Willow was slightly traumatised by her brother (Samson) who was returned (himself slightly traumatised) as a kitten for a while. Cats do not always get on and new cats have to be slowly introduced into new environments where other cats already have their territory. Cats can be terribly suspicious of one another when initially familiarising themselves and the already ensconced cat might attack the new cat as it is seen as a territorial intruder.

Previously, left alone, Willow was the most peaceful of kittens. She then learned to fight back in self-defence and became a bit of a tomboy. Samson and Willow were often found careering around at full pelt in spectacular scenes of gladiatorial displays, an example of competitive existence indicative of a sibling, territorial sharing problem and masculine dominance. Naturally, Willow escalated and retaliated earning her claws, stripes, spots and ribbons, but gentleness was always her real nature. It was an unfortunate episode in her very young life.

Willow, like Maggie in the Simpsons, does not really purr yet (although this is slowly developing) or say very much at all. As the youngest she is the quickest with the sharpest claws and on very rare occasions can be unnecessarily spiteful, particularly toward her mother, Dinah. We suspect she already has one eye on future Queendom, but long will she have to wait. The flip sympathy side is that as the youngest she can be picked on by the other cats, particularly Iolaus who, as elder half-brother, seems to think it is fair game to pick on his little half-sister.

However, Willow is beginning to relax and is starting to develop her own distinctive greeting voice and style, whilst emitting a deeper power of purr when she is relaxed and in a trusting state. On the rare occasions she is heard talking, she has a quick, high, almost electric, type of meow (her 'prr-prr' means 'Hello'). She lives mainly outdoors now for she loves her roaming freedom. I think her next incarnation is going to be as a fox.

<u>Willow</u>

Skitty kitty

Claws so bright

Sharper than your kitten bite

Prowling around the house and flat

You are a ferocious

Tiger cat.

Invisible!

Tight-curled ball

Sleeping in the bathroom sink,

Spots and stripes

Panthera might –

What will all the little mice think!

A fancy cat…

Well fancy that!

She is a pouncing Minnie-the-Minx!

*

In conclusion: So, to all the cats, past, present and future, that have, do and will, grace our presence we give thanks – with a special dedication and especial appreciation to our present cats for allowing me the experience of becoming a Purr-Doctor in training. On the all important cat contentment continuum they are Happy Cats; to us they are our daily companions and little friends. I am truly grateful to them for being our four living, ringing-singing bowls of beauty and pleasure. They are our waking morning meow-ers, our delightful afternoon carpet comforters and secret midnight conspiratorial chums all rolled into one.

ABOUT THE AUTHOR

Keith Brazil was born in Broadstairs, Kent, England. He trained in Dance Theatre at Laban Trinity Conservatoire, London, and was a founder member of 'Adventures In Motion Pictures' Dance Company. He has worked as a freelance professional dancer, choreographer, teacher, and dance lecturer. Keith has also trained as a Complementary Therapist in Spiritual Healing and Reflexology. He gained a degree in English Studies and is currently engaged in writing a collection of metaphysical and fictional stories, essays, poetry and novels. His first book <u>The Wilderness Diary</u> was published in December 2012. The companion book, <u>Popcorn, Parasites, Precious & Pearls</u>, is due for release Autumn 2013. He lives and works in London.

IN CONSIDERATION OF CATS